Talk **Co**
For if yo
con{

NOR\
in this never-before-published book

~

Ninety per cent of world's woes come from people not knowing themselves, their abilities, their frailties, and even their real strengths. Most of us go almost all the way through life as complete strangers to ourselves.

Just keep one fact in mind. 'There are no hopeless situations, just hopeless people'. Never, never, give up, as Churchill once advised. The more profoundly you believe in yourself, the more surely you will be happy and satisfied in your life.

Take control of your life, *confidently*.

~

'...the most widely read inspirational writer of our time.'
Christian Herald, Boston, USA

Publisher's Note

1st International edition

The material presented in these pages is being published as a book for the first time ever, anywhere in the world.

The book is based on these writings of Norman Vincent Peale which were scattered at several places and never published as a book.

In the last few years a great deal of effort and energy were invested in collecting and editing Peale's writings on the subject of confidence development, self-esteem and success. This book is a result of those sustained efforts.

THE POWER OF CONFIDENCE

NORMAN VINCENT PEALE

DELHI | MUMBAI | HYDERABAD

ISBN : 978-81-222-0510-7

The Power of Confidence

Subject: Self-Help / Personal Growth / Self Esteem

© 2010 Peale Centre for Christian Living

1st Published 2012
6th Printing 2016

Published in arrangement with
Guideposts, USA

Published by
Orient Paperbacks
(A division of Vision Books Pvt. Ltd.)
5A/8 Ansari Road, New Delhi-110 002
www.orientpaperbacks.com

Printed at Artxel, Noida

Contents

1 Become All You Can Be ... 9
2 How to Handle Tough Times ... 37
3 You Can Overcome Any Problem ... 65
4 Positive Changes for Success ... 107
5 Enthusiasm: What It can Do for You ... 123
6 Courage: Finding Your Strength in Troubled Times ... 149
7 How to Make a New Start ... 159
8 Trust: Believe in Yourself. Believe in the Future ... 187

What you become depends on you.

Chapter 1

Become all you can be

A man of words and not of deeds
is like a garden full of weeds.

— *Anonymous*

The more I work with people, the more I'm convinced that only a few root causes produce all of the negative results in our lives. Chief among these causes is low self-esteem. Among school children, the bully is always someone who has a low opinion of himself. The fears, neuroses, and behavioural disorders of adults who seek counselling are rooted more in this cause than in any other single cause.

All of us need to develop a strong, healthy self-esteem. There's no winning in life without this key ingredient. And no matter how poorly you regard yourself at this moment, you can change your opinion of yourself.

Now, there is a great difference between healthy self-esteem and unhealthy pridefulness. The first is based on God's opinion of you and His love for you. The second is simply bloated self-inflation.

The foundation for human self-worth comes from God. The seed of divine nature is planted in every man, woman, and child, giving us priceless worth.

Each person is responsible to nurture and grow that seed. You must listen to your inner censor, give your best, live with enthusiasm, put your mind to work and put your faith in God.

Let Your Censor Be Your Guide

Would you like to know, for certain, whether you are on the right track, doing the right thing in the right way? There is a simple but accurate way to find out.

Do you desire an answer to whether you have it in you to do something really worthwhile? The same test will give you the answer.

Do you want to be sure your thinking and actions are absolutely honest, or whether they are questionable or dishonest? You can know that too, and for sure.

The way to find out these three things about yourself is quite easy. But the test will accurately give you all the facts and completely truthful answers.

Here is the test:

How good, or not so good, do you honestly feel about yourself after you do whatever you do?

To help us keep the faith, God built into each of us something called a censor. Your censor is persistently powerful, always awake, and invariably factual. It tells you clearly whether a thought or action is right or whether it is wrong. It does not deal in 'ifs' or 'buts.' It does not ever argue a matter, or rationalise a decision. Its conclusions are never grey; they are only black or white, that is, wrong or right.

Your censor likes you and is working for you. It wants only success and happiness for you. But it will not compromise and go along with you when something you are thinking and want to do is wrong, or when you don't see why it isn't okay, and argue that everyone else is doing it. The only standard your censor has is simply: Is it right? And the reason it is invariable in its messages to you is that it wants to shield you from failure and from the misery that results from wrong thinking and wrong doing.

Your censor is not a killjoy. It is a *builder* of joy! It is *for* you, not *against* you. It is your friend. And if you listen to its friendly counsel, and accept it as the wise advice that it is, and follow it always, you will have the best in life and be successful as a person.

What happens when you do not heed your censor's sensible counsel? It creates within you a vague, dissatisfied feeling. It may even be a low-grade, but persistent, self-disgust when you commit a wrong, or are presented with an opportunity, but don't think you are up to it and so let it go by, wishing forever after that you had had the nerve to do it.

What really, is this thing I call a 'censor'? Is it conscience? No, I believe it is more basic, for conscience is something acquired by religious teaching, whereas the censor works in even unlearned or irreligious people. It is a natural part of a human being. All are endowed with it. A sensitivity to rightness and wrongness is in all people, for

'Feel Good About Yourself' Test

Harold was a commercial artist and an expert one, too, and made a good income at it. He would accept contracts for sexy pictures that verged on the immoral, a kind of dirty art. And the going rate for these off-colour drawings, he said, was higher than the pay for the decent kind. Then Harold started coming to me. He once asked me how one could be sure which was right in a decision between right and wrong. 'My friends argue with me,' he said, 'drawing a distinction between what they call "the old-time, out-dated morality" and "the new morality." 'What shall I do?' he asked. 'Is there any rule I can go by.'

I suggested that he might test all decisions by asking, 'What would God do?'

'But I'm not in the same league with God,' Harold protested. 'He has understanding and strength far beyond me. Isn't there another test that is more my style?'

So I gave him the 'Feel good about yourself' test: 'If you don't feel good yourself doing it, then it is wrong. But, if you have a good feeling about yourself doing that thing, then you can believe it to be right.' This seemed to satisfy him as reasonable.

The next day at the office, his supervisor assigned him a new job. 'Make the picture a really sexy come-on, Harold. You know how to titillate the reader. Pour it on, boy!' So saying, he left Harold sitting at his drawing board thinking. At once, Harold knew how he would feel about himself if he executed this assignment. And he knew for certain that for him to draw this illustration would definitely be wrong.

He arose and went to the supervisor. 'Fred, I can't do it.' Then he explained about his commitment to God, and how he knew this would be wrong. The boss said, 'But you have done this kind of work before.' Harold explained that loyalty to God, for him, meant living by a higher ethical standard — doing only what he thought was right.

'Harold,' the boss said, 'I understand and admire your honesty, so I'll assign this job to someone else. But, son, I'll have to let you go. I'm sorry.' With that, Harold put on his jacket, went home and explained to his wife, Janet, that he had been fired. She said, 'Honey, I'm proud of you. Let's have faith that God will take care of us and guide us.' As days faded into weeks, it became hard-going for Harold and Janet.

But they just tightened their belts and prayed with ever-deepening faith. Then one day, a man from an employment agency telephoned Harold. 'There is a big job calling for a top-flight illustrator,' he said, 'and you have been strongly recommended for it.' It was to do a work of high quality. Later, Harold found out that the person who had recommended him was the boss who had discharged him. So he went to see him. 'Thanks, Fred. That's mighty decent of you. Why?'

'Because I like you, Harold, and you do excellent work. Besides...' he hesitated, 'you're quite a man, son. You have guts; you're real. Good luck, Harold.'

'Did I ever feel good walking out of Fred's office!' Harold told me later. 'I sure felt great about myself that I kept the faith.'

even the most ignorant have a bell that rings inside them when they act meanly or dishonestly or cruelly to a fellow being, or when they shy away from an opportunity.

Most of what I know about the censor, I learned from Smiley Blanton, a brilliant psychiatrist who had studied under the great Sigmund Freud. Smiley and I worked together for years, helping people solve their problems. He talked about the censor often, and I came to trust him as an authority on the matter. But if you don't want to trust me or a Freudian psychiatrist, consult a dictionary. There, you will find, in plain English, a definition something like this one: Censor — the force that represses unacceptable ideas, impulses and feelings and prevents them from reaching the conscious mind.

Remember that, in one way, the censor is like a good parent. It disapproves when you are wrong, and sounds a warning. But it is important to remember that, like your God-created parents, the God-created censor hates the sin — but continues to love the sinner.

At any rate, the extent to which we react and respond to the inner censor pretty much determines whether we become happy people and attain the stature of success we desire.

Action Steps

1. Test your actions and decisions each day by asking yourself the following: 'Do I feel good — or uneasy and uncomfortable — about what I've done?'

2. List your good actions on one sheet of paper and your poor actions on another. Continue to do this until you develop a natural instinct for making right, ethical decisions.

Give Life Your All

You are never going to become all you can be if you continue to do less than your best.

As an illustration of the best that lies within you, may I tell you the story of one person who consulted me? Her name was Miss Lou. Everyone in the small Mississippi town where she lived called her that, she told me. Hearing that I was scheduled to speak in Mobile, Alabama, she made an appointment to talk with me.

She was a little lady — charming, well-dressed, cultured. Her gracious personality, lovely accent, and courtesy marked her at once as being of the finest type of old-fashioned southern gentlewomen of the yesterdays. She was all apologies for 'bothering' me with her problem.

But she was direct and came quickly to the point, which indicated she had sharp mental organisation and was businesslike. Her husband had died recently. They had always lived well, though without ostentation. He had been a leading businessman in the community and was well respected. They had servants 'and all that' and life went along pleasantly. Then one night, she said, 'my sweetheart went home to Heaven peacefully, but oh so suddenly.'

'In the days following, I had to reorganise my life,' she continued. 'I found that I had little money to live on. This realisation was a shock. My husband had never discussed business with me, and I don't think I would have grasped it if he had. I found that he had debts to be paid off. When everything was settled, I realised that I must find something to do.

'But Dr. Peale, I just can't do anything. I've never had to work, and have no training at all. More than that, I have no ability or talent.' She gave a deep sigh. 'Guess I'm useless and a total failure. I'm just a no-account woman of the "lavender and old lace" generation, bound to end up in the poor house.'

'But I assume you are a believer. Are you a Christian?' I asked.

'Oh yes, indeed. I have gone to church every Sunday.'

'And, at church, have you learned who you are?'

Puzzled by the question, she replied, 'Do you mean that God created us, and we are His children?' she asked.

I told her about a framed sign I saw behind the counter of a drugstore. It pictured a little boy saying,

'I like me because God made me and He don't make no junk.'

and I added, 'Guess, as such, we should have self-esteem.'

'Oh yes I realize that. I've been putting myself down too much.'

Then I told her: 'One of the first things we must learn is what resources are built into us. A normal self-esteem is good for us. It is the belief that, with God's guidance and help, we have what it takes to handle any situation we may face, and do so creatively.

'So, Miss Lou, start thinking positively. Muster up your self-esteem and draw upon your faith.'

'I must be a poor believer,' she said.

'Correct that, Miss Lou,' I said gently. 'Instead, say this: "I am a real believer in the Lord and in myself." ' Dutifully, she repeated that affirmation, word for word. 'Aren't I a good pupil?' she asked demurely. I liked her.

'Now let's canvas the field of prospective jobs. How about working in a women's store, or a flower shop, making arrangements. Do you have skill in painting or handicraft of any kind?'

'I've never done any of those things,' she replied.

'Can you think of anything you like to do?' I asked.

'Well, I make pretty good candy,' she replied. 'I will send you a box.'

'That's great!' I replied, warming to the possibilities. 'You can turn a room in your home into a shop and sell that candy to neighbours and tourists.'

'Oh, Dr Peale, I couldn't do that. I'll give the candy to my neighbours, not sell it. To make money from them would be discourteous.'

I proceeded to give her a lecture on free enterprise: Selling a good product for a fair price is just good business.

Finally, I won her promise to think about opening a shop to sell candy.

A few days later, I received the promised box at home, and the candy was terrific. I sent her a telegram ordering several boxes for friends, and insisted upon paying. She went into business and called her shop, 'The Sweetest Spot on Highway 56.' But more important, she became an even greater personality success.

Little Miss Lou became enthusiastically involved in life in her town. Her activity was such that two or three years later, the U.S. Chamber of Commerce recognised this little self-effacing woman as one of the ten outstanding Americans for that year.

Miss Lou did not make a fortune selling candy, nor did her little shop grew into a national enterprise. What did happen was that a defeated person, a negative individual, changed into a positive, believing woman and a victorious human being. She used to write me joyous, enthusiastic letters and said over and over, 'It's all so wonderful! I felt so bad about myself, and you taught me instead how to feel good about myself.' The good possibilities within this person were lying dormant under feelings of uselessness. But when they were released, life was magnificently different. And that miracle of change can happen to anyone.

The trouble about telling such a story is that you may think, *That is wonderful about Miss Lou but, as for me, I'm just an ordinary person.* So was she, and that is precisely the way she talked. But she changed her thoughts about herself, she got outside of herself, got above her negativism. She was a hopeless and seemingly helpless widow. But she listened to the idea of what it took to change basic attitudes, and she went about changing herself. She got to where she could feel good about herself. And having mastered this lesson in the importance of giving life her all, she did not foolishly return to her previous lack of self-esteem, but continued happily to the end as a believer in God and in herself.

I shall ever remember Miss Lou, for her experience proved that all of us have within ourselves a powerful resource by which defeat may be turned into achievement.

Action Steps
1. Remove the negatives from your vocabulary. Instead of saying, 'I cannot,' in response to challenges and difficulties, say, 'I can.'
2. Increase your self-esteem by looking into a mirror each morning and repeating, 'If God is for me, who can be against me?'
3. Your first priority should be to believe that God has a good opinion of you and next, that you have a good opinion of yourself. Do not rely on praise from others to give you confidence.

Do Only What Is Right

If the absence of trouble resulting from wrong actions means something to you, if the inexpressible satisfaction of feeling good about yourself appeals to you, follow this — *Do only what you know to be right!*

This is one of the safest principles in this world for keeping things from going bad and making things go well for you. People who think that this concept is outmoded, or who assume they can have an easy, bendable moral attitude and get away with it forever, do find otherwise. Adherence to a moral code does not guarantee sweetness and light. It does promise an enveloping feeling of rightness much more surely than the contrary view of ethics.

An example of what can happen when someone departs from the moral code was brought home to me recently. On a speaking trip, my wife, Ruth, and I were staying in a hotel in Columbus, Ohio. From our room, the panorama of the city spread out before us. Standing at a window, I saw something that sparked a tragic memory. It was a low group of grey buildings. Calling Ruth to come and look, I said, 'That is the old Ohio State Penitentiary. A good man I knew, with a weak streak in his make-up, served a lengthy term over there years ago. He was a nice fellow, brought up in a fine family, but fell for the idea that morals, like styles, are changeable.'

Everyone foresaw for him a brilliant career. He graduated *summa cum laude* from college. He was a particularly engaging fellow whom everyone liked and trusted. And he became a top officer of the local bank. People were urging him to run for the state legislature. He would be a 'shoo-in', it was said. He had everything going for him, but ...!

He married a beautiful girl from Chicago. She had big ideas socially and ran up large accounts at department stores and specialty shops. In short, she was an expensive lass. But she was most attractive, and people indulged her. His good salary was stretched to the breaking point. The wife opted for trips to Chicago, New York, Paris, and that did it. He couldn't bring himself to deny her anything, and she didn't give finances any thought.

So, to get more money, he invested in the stock market. But the perverse market went down, and he had to get more money from somewhere. But where? One night, in the bank, a thought came. A thought should be carefully scrutinised when it is unusual, for the wrong thought can result in a sorry action. The thought was: *Nobody will know if I borrow some cash for a few days. I will recover in the market and quickly put the money back.*

But, being an honest banker and a moral man, he indignantly repulsed the thought. But another night it came again, and another and another. Finally, one night, he put out his hand and did as the thought had suggested. The deed was done!

Then the bank examiner came. After much publicity, the gates of the penitentiary clanged shut behind a good banker who was put there because he had trifled with a bad thought and compromised the moral code in which he believed, but did not believe enough.

This is, I admit, an extreme illustration and a highly dramatic one. Others don't get caught. They seem to get away with it. But someone knows! The censor knows; it never forgets, and it continuously torments. And why? Because it represents the good in every human being. And the good, for some reason known only to the Creator, will not tolerate being flouted.

Action Steps

1. Develop a personal moral code on which you can base all your decisions. Write it down and adhere to it faithfully.
2. Seek opportunities to reinforce your self-esteem. Volunteer in a local nursing home or hospital, teach a Sunday school class, help a shut-in. Doing something for someone else will help your self-esteem to grow.
3. Evaluate your job or your life's responsibilities. If unreasonable demands required your participation in actions that make you uneasy, look for alternatives.

Believe In Yourself

You will never become all you can be until you develop a good self-esteem. As long as you have a bad feeling or even a doubtful self-appraisal, you will lack a feeling of self-worth. The cultivation of a normal feeling of self-esteem will do wonders for you. I know, for I've experienced it myself and I've seen it happen to many people.

I realise fully the problems some people have. But when one stops thinking of obstacles, and starts thinking of his own potentialities, and, with God's help, throws himself into his task, he will come through.

Low self-esteem seems to be a widespread problem. In fact, some educators believe that many teenagers who go for drugs, sex, even violence and suicide are not basically bad kids, but the victims of low self-esteem.

A child at birth, I believe, is positive. A baby instinctively knows it has only to do two things to get anything it wants: cry or coo. Then everyone runs to do its bidding. But some children are born into negative families. And because a child is extremely sensitive to his environment, he unconsciously absorbs the negativism of the home. Accordingly, so it is said by education experts, by the time the child is in elementary school, he has a strong disbelief in his ability and has developed an inferiority attitude: a low self-esteem.

If, later, a young person has enough force of character to forge ahead despite self-doubt, achievement is accomplished with much greater expenditure of energy and sometimes results in an early breakdown. In such a case, a person is deprived of the full joy of life.

What is self-esteem? It means to like yourself, to have a good feeling about you as a person. Because it is the censor that produces bad or good feelings, depending on your wrong or right actions, it follows that to have self-esteem, you must do right. It also follows, as night follows day, that if you have low self-esteem, the simple — and only — way to have a high self-esteem is to do right.

Now, as you may know, I'm somewhat of an expert on low self-esteem. When I was a young boy, I had almost no self-esteem at all. I was painfully bashful. I'm not sure why. Maybe my dear mother had something to do with it. I hesitate to criticise her because she seemed so perfect. But she constantly told me, 'Norman, you must be somebody!' She wanted to be proud of me, and she constantly compared me to others. That worked as a prod, but it also crowed me.

Then, I was very skinny. I was mortified because I was so thin. So I consumed thousands of milkshakes. (And they had their effect. By the time I was in my 30s, I weighed 185 pounds!) But, as a child, I was miserable, just miserable.

Thanks to the help of some wonderful people, I was able to overcome the low opinion I had of myself. If I can do it, you can, too.

∽

I once spoke to 4000 school teachers. The man who served as my host was the superintendent of schools in a city in Missouri. I asked him, 'If you were a non-educator making a speech to 4000 school teachers, what would you tell them?'

'Well,' he replied, 'I would like you to tell them what we asked you down here to tell them.'

'And what is that?' I asked.

'Tell them that they are greater people than they think they are. Tell them that they have to find themselves. If they don't, their students won't find themselves. Urge them to believe in themselves.'

And then he added: 'Let me tell you about one of my teachers. He has a brilliant mind and superb training. He has several advanced degrees in education. I was surprised that he came back to Missouri to teach but was, of course, delighted to have him. I assigned him to one of the best opportunities I had available in the public-school system. But some weeks later he came to me and said, "I would like you to transfer me."

' "Why?" I asked.

' "Because," he said, "I'm frightened of these students. I cannot establish rapport with them. As a result, I am not helping them adequately. And I feel inadequate." Despoundently he admitted, "I guess I don't really believe in myself."

'I was disturbed by the teacher's request, and arranged the transfer. Six months later, he was back again, once more asking to be transferred, again complaining, "I do not feel adequate; I do not believe in myself." '

The superintendent then realised that basic action was required. He began to talk to this teacher about God.

But this superintendent wasn't worried by such matters; besides, he was dealing man-to-man with a troubled human being. He said to the young teacher: 'Look, Jim, perhaps I can tell you why you do not believe in yourself.

The Best Air-conditioner

I once called an air-conditioner company and asked if the firm handled a certain make, which I had become convinced was the best in the business. My high opinion of this product was based on the perfect air conditioning in a hotel room where I stayed overnight in super-hot weather. So I was sold on this make and model.

The company sent one around with a salesman. 'Is this the best air conditioner that's made, and will it give perfect performance?' I asked.

The salesman took his time answering, and then surprised me by asking, 'What is your definition of perfect?'

I stumbled in reply. 'Why... I guess I mean... can it be counted on to give the best service always and for a long time.'

Well, he then gave me a moderate, sensible explanation of air conditioners, climate variation and humidity control, which amounted to this: 'We think this make and model is one of the best available and its record of performance seems to be pretty good.' He told me that the one I had encountered in a motel must have been fine-tuned by someone who knew what he was doing. 'But do you know how to fine-tune an air conditioner?' he asked. When I showed doubt, he gave me a patient course of instructions.

'Dr. Peale,' he said, 'all well-known makes are good. Of course, we think ours is tops. But it's probably not better an air conditioner than I am a man, and I try to be a good man. I don't really aspire to be the best man in the world, but I do believe that this is a good air conditioner. And if you take care of it and handle it right, I think it will be giving you satisfaction ten years from now.'

Well, I looked with admiration at that quiet, sensible, honest man. Actually, I bought him rather than the air conditioner. It's long past ten years, and the air conditioner is still going strong. While we were completing the purchase, we got to talking, and he said, 'I have self-respect, and I resolved that I would do only what I believe to be right. By doing that, I always feel good about myself.'

Noticing my Rotary pin, he told me he was a member of the Rotary Club. A long while later, I met a member of his club. I asked if he knew this air-conditioner salesman. 'Do I know him! Well, I should say so. He is one of the most decent and honest men I've ever known. And he is a genuinely happy person.'

So, as this man demonstrates, doing what you know to be right seems to pay off — in increasing your chances of success and happiness.

It's because you don't really believe in anything higher than yourself. You are just a little person, mixed up. Now,' he went on, 'I am going to try to lead you to God, and I shall stay with you until you find Him. For when you do, you will feel a wonderful inner strength and support. I'll guarantee that you will believe in yourself.'

What a beautiful thing that is — a school superintendent leading a brilliant teacher to the great Teacher. And when he found the great Teacher, he did find himself completely, so much so that the superintendent told me that the young man is one of the best he has in his system.

Every person will do well to emphasize that he or she is a somebody endowed by God with a good personality and abilities. Actually, you are a unique person. Among all the millions, there is no one in this world quite like you. You are one of a kind. You are yourself; you are a child of God; you are immortal. So drop that low self-esteem. Think of yourself as a God-blessed person, and you will have a good feeling about yourself. And that good feeling will be justified.

And do you know something? Other people will have a good feeling about you. But exercise care not to become cocky. Always remain humble. In fact, never cease to remember that what you are is a gift from God.

Action Steps

1. You are greater than you think you are. Accept this as fact, and you will live up to the potential you were born with.

2. Set aside 15 minutes a day for a spiritual quiet time. Use that time to read, pray, and allow God's guidance to work for good in your life.
3. When faced with obstacles, remember: you are bigger than your problem, and optimism and faith will help you find a solution.

Think! Always Think!

The next step in becoming all you can be is this: Think! Always think!

Living on an emotional level, getting mad, getting even, really showing them, making a pile and cleaning up no matter how you do it — all these are emotional attitudes, and do not reflect sound thinking. And it's doubtful that anyone ever feels really good about himself with such emotions activating and motivating him. I'm not about to say that it's bad to make money, if possessing it isn't the main thing in life.

Money is only a tool, a medium of exchange, or, as a prominent European business women said, 'The only value of money is to make the wheel of business go round. But to have it just to "feel the gold in your fingers" is vulgar.'

Having operated some business enterprises, I know the relationship of income to expenses, and that a fair profit on a good value is basic. But, also, I know that greed never made anyone look in the mirror and really feel proud of himself.

The wisest document in the world does not say that money is the root of all evil. It says that the *love* of money is evil. There is quite a difference between the two concepts.

The mind, when supplied steadily with unhealthy emotions like greed, jealousy, and hate, will finally take on the colour of the thoughts these emotions generate. For example, when one's mind becomes filled with hate thoughts, which is a sick emotion, it loses its power to think with clarity, precision, and objectivity. It gets so used to turning over its basic hates, churning them with vitriolic emotion, that it cannot achieve the remarkable efficiency for which this amazing mental machine is intended.

Quite apart from religious or moral concerns, the emotion of hate acts like a destructive corrosive element in the mind itself, and actually prevents it from formulating and developing ideas, which is one of its basic functions. But when such emotions are flushed out of the mind, then sharp mental processes take their natural course and produce creative ideas.

In my travels, I encountered a young businessman who told me that he experienced happiness 'like never before' when he let God into his life. It seems he had read *The Power of Ethical Management*, written by Dr. Kenneth Blanchard and myself.

In that book, we outline an ethical check as follows:
1. Is it legal? Will I be violating either civil law or company policy?
2. Is it balanced? Is it fair to all concerned in the short term as well as the long term? Does it promote win-win relationships?
3. How will it make me feel about myself? Will it make me proud? Would I feel good if my decision was published in the newspaper? Would I feel good if my family knew about it?

This man said the test of how one feels about himself was completely new to him. But it did coincide with persistent inner feelings he had experienced about himself, a sort of gnawing dissatisfaction and even distaste for his lifestyle. He had never had any religious or ethical training, and indeed had been raised in a totally irreligious family. But he still had 'bad feelings when he did bad things and good feelings when he did good things.' I took this to mean that the inner censor had been working in his consciousness as a natural phenomenon. As a result, together with a study of our book, he was seemingly on the way to developing an ethical personal-life management.

~

Let me tell you about an acquaintance of mine — a man who could have easily grown up resenting the world because of the tough breaks he received early in life.

His name is Thomas Monaghan. And I recently had an opportunity to meet with this delightful man.

Following the death of their father in 1941, young Thomas and his brother, Jimmy, were placed in a orphanage. Although only nine years old at the time, Thomas was a big dreamer with even bigger ambitions. He was lucky enough to have a friend who encouraged him to shoot for the stars. Her name was Sister Mary Berarda.

According to Thomas, right from the start, Sister Berarda supported him 'Okay, Tom,' she would say, 'Have faith in God, have faith in yourself — then go out and do it! You can be anything you want to be.'

The kind-hearted nun also encouraged Thomas to read books and articles about people such as Henry Ford and McDonald's restaurant founder Ray Kroc. Her goal was to show the boy that success could be his, regardless of his background. The boy listened, and her words stayed with him as he grew up.

Thomas worked hard. In the early 1960s, he bought a pizza parlour. Business went well, and he bought a second pizzeria. Then he had an idea: He decided to deliver his pizzas, and guarantee that they would arrive hot within 30 minutes. This was a new concept in pizza delivery: the convenience of being at home and enjoying pizza fresh from the oven.

Thomas hit on something and, little by little, he expanded his business. By 1973 he had 60 franchises. He realized that he was on his way to becoming the type of self-made man he had read about as a boy.

As he grew more successful, his thoughts turned to his wise friend and teacher, Sister Berarda. He felt ashamed that he had not talked with her, or thanked her for what she had done for him. After checking around, he found that she lived in a retirement home. He hurried to see her. Nearly 40 years had passed.

'I did what you said, Sister,' he told her. 'I followed your advice; I had faith in myself. I'm a self-made man.'

'Yes, you're successful,' she said proudly, 'and I always knew you could do it. But Tom, there is really no such thing as a self-made man.'

Sister Berarda's words made Thomas realize that in his quest for success he had let God take second place to his faith in himself. He wasn't self-made man; he was a God-made man.

From that day on, Thomas began to change his life. He prayed daily. As his business continued to grow (Domino's Pizza now has over 4700 franchises around the world), Thomas grew spiritually, keeping God at the forefront of all that he did.

Today, Thomas has ministerial staff at Domino's Pizza's world headquarters. On a voluntary basis, employees can attend daily church services, holiday services, and a weekly Bible study.

Thomas's dedication to the Lord shines through in his actions and his attitudes. All of his employees are familiar with his five lifelong priorities, which are, in order: paying attention to the spirtual side of his life; caring for his family; keeping his mental state sharp; keeping himself physically fit; and watching over his finances. He recommends these priorities to all his employees. I was not at all surprised to learn that there are Domino's Pizza employees whose lives have been changed since they started working for Thomas.

In getting to know God, Thomas Monaghan got to know himself. That's what enabled him to set the priorities in his life; that's what has enabled him to be such a successful and admired businessman.

Action Steps

1. Analyse your goals in life. Question their value. Do you worship gods of lust, power, or money — or do you give greater value to your spiritual well-being? Choose your priorities in life and then proceed to pursue them.

2. As a reminder of your personal moral code, ask yourself the following questions before you act on a decision: Is it legal?; Is it balanced and fair in the short term, as well as in the long term?; and Do I feel proud of myself? Do I want the world to know about this? Write these questions on an index card and keep it within easy reach.

3. If you harbour hatred or resentment toward anyone, pray for this person. In time, your prayers will remove the hate, leaving you emotionally and mentally free to concentrate on more-productive activities.

Chapter 2

How to handle tough times

The great powerful truth:
for every problem,
there is an answer.

*D*o you really know how to deal successfully with difficulties?

Do you handle things with a sense of control, knowing that you can cope with the vicissitudes and circumstances of everyday existence? Or do you tend to fall apart, and become depressed and hopeless about your situation? These are important questions for us all.

For anyone whose life is confused, disorganised, frustrated, or lacking in energy and vitality, the best thing to do is to get healed of such negatives and become filled with positive faith.

You might say, 'But you don't know how tough my life is. I have real problems!'

I am not unaware of how much heartache and struggle there is in human existence. How could I be? Recently, I read more than one hundred letters from the mail that comes to me — broken families, abuse, runway children, drugs, disease, sin, alcoholism, failure, unemployment, loneliness, bereavement. If these letters were put together and published in a book, it would run the gamut of human problems.

But many people who are going through tragic circumstances manage to get hold of a solid faith that helps them achieve victory.

This chapter is intended to help you handle problems instead of allowing them to make you worried and fear-filled. With this book, the obstacles you face will only be obstacles to overcome.

As you incorporate these inspirational ideas into your daily routine, you will begin to look at problems — and their solutions — creatively and positively. and the most amazing things will begin to happen.

Take control of your life, now, and enjoy the adventure of solving your problems, even in the toughest of times.

Lift Your Spirits

You realize, do you not, that the most powerful force in this universe is a positive thought properly used. Outward circumstances or conditions do not determine what our lives become nearly so much as do the thoughts that dominate our minds. *No one can ever overcome anything until his thoughts are creative and positive.*

It is important that you lift your mind to a higher level. Mentally, as you raise your mind above the defeats and conflicts you face, your personality will receive help from God in the form of clear thinking, resolute reaching out toward happiness, deeper understanding, and renewed strength. When your thoughts are in confusion, you live in an unreal world, and you cannot see your way up and out of it.

A man who once came asking for help with a personal problem said, 'Ordinarily, I can think my way out of a difficulty, but my spirits are so low that I have become extraordinarily depressed. I seem to be surrounded by grotesque shadows so that familiar faces and situations have become unreal world because my thoughts are depressed. If I could only get my spirits lifted, I believe I could see my way through this matter. Then I would have the courage and insight to face this problem and overcome it. Please tell me how to get my spirits lifted.' I suggested the steps described below. He applied them and soon was in command of his life and problems.

Monitor Your Moods

Once in a while, I read the stock-market reports, though my chief reading in any newspaper is first, the sport pages, then the front page, then the editorials. Occasionally, on the financial page there is a chart showing how stocks have gone up and down. I discovered that whenever the graph goes down, people get worried, and whenever it goes up, they are happy.

Well, everything in this universe moves according to a graph, according to rhythm. This is true not only of the stock market but also of human moods. A person need not be overly concerned when his mood drops a little; that is normal. Nor need he be overly elated when his mood rises. That, too, is normal. Our present consideration is when your mood goes down and stays down. Then is when you need real help. Then you need an answer to the question, 'How can I get my spirits lifted?'

Think of the Sun

In moods of discouragement or despair, never forget that the sunshine will ultimately come back, that its absence never is permanent. Hang on to your faith, knowing that soon you will rise into the sunshine again.

Nothing can happen in a human life that is so bad that the sunlight will not shine again, if you lift up your eyes from whence cometh your help. Remember all the good things that God has done for you in the past. That is the sunlight of the past. Then visualise — and never let the visualisation become dim — the sunlight of the future and all the good that God will do for you and your loved ones in the future. Always remember the sunlight of the past, and the sunlight of the future, in the dark days.

Clear your Mind

Another element in getting your spirits lifted is to empty your mind of all negative thoughts: all hateful, apprehensive, fearful, and evil thoughts. Note how much better you feel, and how your spirits have lifted.

You can hardly expect your spirits to soar, when they are weighed down with resentment, self-pity and ill will. If you go round and round in a circle, carrying these negative thoughts, your spirits are held down. The mind of an average person can be like a defective phonograph record I possess from my early days. I bought it in Hawaii

'What Is Your Secret?'

On the west coast of Florida, I met an old Scotsman, one of those philosophical characters from whom you can learn a great deal. He was in charge of the swimming pool at the hotel where I was staying, and I got into a conversation with him.

He said, 'There are two things that will make you live twenty years longer: sunlight and water. Go into a pool every day for thirty minutes, and you will live twenty years longer.'

'But,' he continues, 'you also must have sunlight. This locality (the South) is the greatest place. I stay here the year round because we have sunlight. The human spirit perishes without the sun; that is why you find so many neurotics in northern climates. I once sailed on a vessel for three weeks and did not see a crack in the clouds. The crew became morose and gloomy and sick. But I had a secret that kept me up.'

'What was your secret?' I asked, interested in his philosophy.

'Every day,' his answer was, 'I would go out when the clouds hung low and do two things. One, I remembered the golden sunlight of days past, and two, I thought of the golden sunlight that would come when those clouds had rolled away. Thus, I made my own sunlight. I distilled it in my heart. I manufactured it in my mind. I could feel it warming my bones, entering into the essence of my being.' So concluded my philosophical Scots friend.

and it is a typical Hawaiian song. But there is a defective spot in this record and, when the needle gets to that spot, the record plays the phrase in the song over and over. After a while, it gets monotonous. Some people's minds go round and round in their self-pity, their fears and their hates, so they never get their problems solved. Their spirits never go up, and the mind refuses to work with the efficiency of which it is capable.

So what must we do? We must lift up our eyes unto the high places, getting our minds off destructive attitudes toward other people. We must get our minds off ourselves, our hates, our failures, and our resentments, and lift them up to the high places. We must look fearlessly at all the gloom and remind ourselves that it is not permanent. We must lift up our minds to God and let faith pour down into us. Then our spirits will rise like birds on the wing; then life will be fascinating and good every day, all our days.

Handle Your Mistakes

The young man, sitting in my office, was completely dejected and depressed. He was beset by an exasperating frustration. 'Why did I do it?' he kept asking, as though unable to believe he could have been so stupid. 'How could I make such a terrible mistake? What is wrong with me? I had the opportunity of a lifetime and I blew it!'

This 29-year-old man had been dropped from a good position with a big firm because, he told me, he had made one serious mistake. I thought it strange that a company would discharge a man for one mistake. But

I remembered the words of a prominent businesswoman, president of her company, who said, 'He who stumbles twice on the same stone deserves to break his own neck.' Which is to say that (in her opinion) a person should be allowed one mistake, but not two. Thank God the Lord allows us so many of them!

This young man was so beside himself, so distraught, that he excited my deepest sympathy and I conveyed to him the following suggestions on how he might learn to handle mistakes in the future.

Learn From Your Mistakes

Every mistake has positive qualities and characteristics. It is a developmental experience, for one thing: something that helps us to grow. It is partly through trial and error that we develop judgement and become mature. A mistake is not something to complain about, or to be ashamed of. It is a great teacher.

A west coast minister, a friend of mine, told me about a 19-year-old boy who came to see him in great desperation. The boy sat with his head in his hands, groaning. He blurted out to this minister, 'For God's sake, pastor, help me. I was smoking pot for months, and now I'm on crack. I was told by some stupid jerks that it would help me live in another world. Well, it's another world, all right, a lousy world. I'm all messed up inside. Can you help me? I know I've made a terrible mistake. But if I can only get myself straightened out, I'll never go back to doing drugs again.'

The pastor, being a wise man, showed the boy love, respect and esteem. And, because he was a wise man, he also referred the boy to doctors who could help him overcome his chemical dependency. 'And,' he told this boy, 'through faith in God, you can create a chemistry within you that will give you a "high" unlike any drug known to man. Then you will truly "come alive."'

Replace Error With Truth

There is always the problem of repeated mistakes that stem from an inner tendency in a person. This is an issue in life that all of us must understand and deal with. If a person's mental or spiritual condition is not right, often times he becomes error prone. There is an old hymn with these words in it, 'Prone to error, Lord, I feel it.' The more error you have within you, the more mistakes you will make, and the more you will do things wrong. The correction for this is, of course, truth, the truth that comes from God. The person who fills his mind with truth will finally cast out error and, to the extent to which he does this, he will have a marvellous life.

Have you developed the ability to distinguish between that which is error and that which is truth? Don't try to make error into truth by rationalization, because it's not possible. Error is error and truth is truth, and never the twain shall meet. So the issue is: What is to dominate you, truth or error?

He who stumbles twice
on the same stone
deserves to break his neck.

Eliminate the Cause

Error causes mistakes, sometimes serious mistakes. And each of us, in greater or lesser degrees, destroys himself or herself to the extent that error dominates him. Take a sheet of paper and write down the really serious mistakes that you've made in your lifetime. You will probably see that every one of them was caused by error that was within you. The question is how can you eliminate the error.

I was with a man the other day who told me, 'I've had a wonderful spiritual experience and I'd like to tell you about it.' I thought perhaps he was going to tell me he was a converted drunk or a converted thief, or that he'd been running around with someone else's wife and had stopped. But this man's difficulty had been of a different kind. 'I was what you'd call a good man,' he said. 'I didn't lie; I didn't get drunk; I didn't do immoral things. But, I was just plain dumb.'

'Oh,' I said, 'that couldn't be.'

'Yes,' he said, 'I did stupid things, and just the wrong things so many times, that I got hopeless and depressed about myself. Then I read in your books that anybody can change just about anything in his life, if he'll turn his life over to God. Most of the people you told about were those whose sins or weaknesses had gotten them into trouble. You didn't tell about my type. I just wanted greater capacity to live and to do my job better.

'So,' he continued, 'I prayed, saying to the Lord, "Please drive out the error and confusion in me, and fill me with Your truth and Your understanding." And the Lord answered my prayer. Now I have a grasp on problems I never had before. I find that the number of mistakes I make has been greatly reduced, and I have a new sense of control over my life.'

Un-Limit Yourself

I would like to ask you a possibly embarrassing question. What are you doing with the marvelous abilities and the extraordinary potential Almighty God built into you? Now there's a question for you! And only you can answer it.

Experts on human nature generally agree that the average person uses but a fraction of the potential mental capacity that he possesses. Some experts fix this at about 10 percent. A few, a very few, raise it to 20 percent. At the highest estimate, most of us are using no more than one-fifth of the potential mental capacity that is ours. Now this is a tragedy. And what is the reason?

Believe in Your Potential

I suppose one reason is that we just haven't adequately developed the potential that is ours. But a second reason is this: we do a terrible thing to ourselves; we actually clamp down upon ourselves self-imposed limitations. A person tells himself, 'Beyond this point, I cannot go.' And then, an even greater tragedy occurs: we come to the point where we're willing to settle for them. 'This is what I am,' one says. 'Might as well accept it and be content.' Some people even go so far as to say, 'It's God's will' — which is blasphemy if I ever heard any, for God never willed that anyone should be less than he can actually be.

Thus, a truly tragic fact that we must face is that many people settle for — and actually practice — their limitations. They practice them so constantly and for so long a time that the limitations become habits. A person comes to be frozen into his limitations much like a polar ship frozen into the Arctic Ocean, so that it cannot move.

Nothing is Impossible

A boy came to me recently and said, 'These things you write about — they may work for you, but they don't work for me.'

'Why should they work for me and not for you?' I asked.

'You aren't the product of a broken family, but I am,' he explained. 'I didn't have a good upbringing.'

I tried to talk to him but like that defective old phonograph record, he kept coming back to the fact that his was a broken family. His mind held onto that idea and wouldn't let it go. My persistence that he surrender to the Lord and live by His message gradually broke through his mental barrier, and he took hold of the idea that nothing is impossible when you have faith.

Oh, occasionally you do run into a person who impresses you as an egotist. This egotism is not pleasant, but neither is the self-depreciation you hear from so many people. How they explain and re-explain how little ability they have! How they affirm their lack of talent! They even declare that they haven't any brains.

What would this world be like if everyone facing a difficulty, a handicap, an infirmity, a weakness, or some other inability, were to sit back and accept his or her circumstances? Everything would come to a standstill.

Everyone has something of a problem or deficiency that could hold him back — could limit him in some way.

The varieties of self-imposed limitations are legion. Particularly widespread, for example, are those that have to do with growing older.

A newspaper reported a story entitled 'Time Is Not Toxic,' based on a conclusion reached by medical specialists and surgeons at a Midwestern clinic.

The Man Who Lost His Legs

Bob Wieland, a man who lost his legs to a landmine in Vietnam, is someone who could have accepted his limitations. But instead he became a champion weight lifter, marathon runner, tri-athlete, motivational speaker, television actor, and an outspoken advocate for those who have no voice: the homeless, the hungry, and the spiritually confused.

Bob's greatest challenge came with a walk across America — propelling himself on padded knuckles — across the entire country to raise money for the hungry.

His handicap was not a hindrance — it was an incentive. It was a stimulus.

'Anyone who thinks that because he or she is getting along in years and expects to experience loss of vigour, debilities, or degenerative disorders, is suffering from a time neurosis, which may be more effective than physical conditions in producing the effect they fear.' In other words, they have a psychologically sick idea that they insist upon perpetuating: that you have to become old and infirm. This is a self-imposed limitation.

Break the Limitation Barrier

Whatever you do, don't spend your life telling the world and yourself that you do not have within you the capacity to live a good life. We cannot conquer the big limitations by our own unaided strength. Faith in God will set us free. He has freed people from shrinking; He has freed them from self-doubt; He has freed them from their sense of inferiority; He has freed them from shyness; He has freed them from being over-awed by life's difficulties; He has freed them from their lusts, from their dishonesties, from their sins. He has freed them from limitations of every kind.

What are you a captive of? Name it, and then turn your life over to God, surrender yourself to Him, and He will set you free! He surely will.

Sunshine Valley

One spring day, Mrs. Peale and I were driving in West Virginia. We came to a crossroads, where a sign pointing to a meandering little road read 'Sunshine Valley.'

Along the way, we met Tommy Martin, a 12-year-old mountain boy, who came sauntering down the road. He wore a floppy hat on his head, boots on his feet, ragged pantaloons on his legs, had bubble gum in his mouth, and carried a fishing rod over his shoulder. A nicer lad I have never met.

We had left our car, for a moment, to sit beside a rushing mountain stream and to listen to the sound of water singing across the rocks and under a bridge. Then Tommy appeared. He was a normal boy with level eyes, no inhibitions, and no special curiosity. He looked us over with a level gaze, apparently deciding he liked us, and said, 'Hi.' Then he asked me, 'Where is your fishing pole?'

I felt humiliated at my failure to conform to pattern. 'Well, come on,' he offered. 'I'll fish for both of us.'

'What are you using for bait, Tommy? Dry flies or lures?'

Chewing mightily, he replied, 'Just plain old worms. They go further.' He pointed to the fish he pulled out of the water. 'That's a brook trout,' he explained. 'You can tell by the spots. Isn't it beautiful?'

Then I asked one of those stupid adult questions. 'Tommy, do you ever worry about anything?' He looked at me with his big, brown eyes and replied with his mountain twang. 'Worry? Shuck! There ain't nothing to worry about!'

Of course, adult life brings with it responsibilities, and we have to live in a world that requires much of us.

There are many things to be concerned about. But isn't it possible, even so, for a human being, no matter what his age, or where his lot is cast, to keep a spirit that is lighthearted and worry free? I wonder.

Now, I certainly do not mean for people to escape from this world, or to become indifferent to the sufferings and struggles of mankind. Nor do I mean developing a careless unconcern with the problems of society.

What I do mean is that we should govern our minds; and that will make us more effective in life, because we are in tune with God!

Fear No More

There are two kinds of fear: normal fear and abnormal fear. Normal fear is necessary for our protection and for the exercise of a sensible caution. But abnormal fear is something altogether different. Sad indeed are the people who walk day and night in the terror of abnormal fear. It is one of the most crippling afflictions of our day, producing painful symptoms, such as depression and anxiety. In some cases, fear can cause actual physical illness.

We are not supposed to be afraid of anything. The only fear we should have is the fear of God and the fear of doing wrong. That is not fear in the sense of being scared; but, rather, it is an awed respect of God and of what is right. We should walk unfraid. But, as that is not easy, we have to consciously build up our faith.

Do what is right, and you will walk unafraid.

Practice Affirmation

You have known some people, no doubt, who have become absolutely fearless. And these are people of profound faith. 'That is what I would like to be,' you may say. 'I am tired of being afraid of illness and of other people and of possible catastrophes. I want to know how to be free of fear always.' The first thing all of us must realize about fear is that most of the things we are afraid of probably will never really happen. If we let our fears dominate, they could cripple our lives.

One absolute and positive way to let go of your fears is to practice the form of prayer known as affirmation: not the prayer of asking, but the prayer of affirming. Believe that God loves you and that He watches over you. Believe that He is taking care of you this very moment and, therefore, you need not be afraid. Do not say, 'O Lord, please deliver me from fear. I am so tired of being upset and anxious.' Rather, affirm that He is already doing it, and you will drop fear.

One of the elders of our church, an intelligent, dedicated man, told me about his experience in the hospital. At one point in his illness, fear gripped him with icy fingers. 'But,' he said, 'I was told that many people were praying for me. So I began to affirm that these prayers were taking effect and that the Lord was hearing my own prayers. And I had a wonderful experience, for, as I affirmed this, all of a sudden every vestige of fear seemed to leave me. I was at peace and rest, and felt absolutely confident.'

Stand Up to Fear

Fear can't be evaded. And it can't be avoided. It has to be met head on. If you're not willing to go to the heart of what it is you are afraid of, that fear will haunt you constantly. President Theodore Roosevelt once said, 'I have often been afraid, but I wouldn't give in to it. I made myself act as though I was not afraid, and gradually my fear disappeared.' Action is the only answer.

Fear of trying something new, after all, is normal. When a child enters a new school, or when a man starts a new job, he is bound to be fearful. But, if he acts with confidence and faith, his fears vanish. And he has that glowing sense of accomplishment that comes with trying something new, and succeeding. I am sure that you can't sit inside a space shuttle and run through a countdown without some feelings of uncertainty. But, if you accept these feelings as normal, you can deal with them.

Let Fear Motivate You

There are two primary forces in this world, fear and faith. Fear can move you to destructiveness or sickness or failure. Only in rare instances will it motivate you to accomplishment. But faith is a greater force. Faith can drive itself into your consciousness and set you free from fear forever.

Solve Your Problem!

Every person has a unique problem, and it is a rather tough problem, too. That problem is life. What are you going to do about it? If you do not know what you are going to do with life, life will do something to you — that is a fact. Either you will master life or life will master you. It is just that simple. Whatever problems you may be facing, you can solve them, if you will trust yourself and believe in your capacity to do it. If you haven't the know-how, you can get it. If you lack the insight, you can find it. If you do not have the wisdom, you can do something about the everyday problems that come with life.

The crowds on the streets of an English cathedral town were going about their daily activities. Suddenly, someone spotted a young woman standing on a narrow edge high on one of the towers of the cathedral. A great crowd gathered below, hushed and horrified.

Policemen at once climbed the tower and attempted to bring her down. A minister came and talked with her, asking that she tell him whatever was on her mind. But, after some 30 minutes of indecision, she flung herself from the tower down to the street. No one found out what problems had driven the woman to her desperate act. But there is one thing she either didn't know, or couldn't comprehend. It is the great, powerful truth that, for every problem, there is an answer.

'That's great,' you say, 'but how do you get it?'

Think Deep Thoughts

Let me ask you something. How long has it been since you've really thought? Thinking, deep thinking, is one of the most painful exertions known to man. We shrink from it. We like to be relieved of the necessity of it. So we think off the top of our heads. And the trouble with those thoughts off the top of our heads is that they do not go down into the depths of poor minds. But, when one gets over the first hurdle and gets into the area where thinking becomes creative, it's an exciting experience.

The Quick and The Dead

John Burroughs, one of the greatest naturalists, said he felt that there are just two classes of people in the world. He said that he didn't mean men and women, or young and old, or rich and poor. The two classes in his mind were what he called 'the quick' and 'the dead.'

By 'the quick,' he meant people who look at the world and see it; people who listen to the world and hear it; people who get a message from it. The quick are people who are sensitised; they send out antennae. They get the meaning of the world. In other words, they are alive, they are alert, they are vibrant. As for 'the dead' people, while they aren't dead physically, they are dead from the standpoint of sensitivity. They never grapple with ideas, or try new ways of doing things. They are dead in the spirit. They live on the surface.

Clear Your Mind

It was during the Korean War, when an American destroyer lay at anchor in Wonsan Harbour, Korea. It was a still, moonlit night. The tide was ebbing. The hour was midnight.

Path Through the Cemetry

Kenneth McFarland, a wonderful speaker, told the story of how fear can be a powerful motivational factor.

A man worked until midnight every night, and customarily walked home afterward.

One beautiful moonlit night, he thought he would walk through the cemetry, rather than around it, because the way was shorter. This he did for several nights, until the moon began to wane. By then he knew the path through the cemetery and, even though it was absolutely dark, he felt he could walk through safely.

But, one night, as he came along the path in the darkness, his feet suddenly went out from under him, and the man found himself grabbing dirt and sliding into a newly dug grave.

He tried his best to get out, but he was too short and the grave was too deep. All he accomplished was to pull a lot of loose dirt down on himself. Being a practical man, he reasoned that the grave diggers would come back the next morning. So he pulled his coat around him, huddled into a corner of the grave and tried to sleep.

An hour later, another wandering citizen came along through the cemetery. All of a sudden this other man slid into the grave — at the other end — and started making futile efforts to climb out.

Finally, as the second man stood contemplating his situation, our first friend, speaking in the darkness, said,

'Boy, you'll never get out that way.' But the second man did — like a shot!

You see, this second man (and for that matter, the first one, too) had the potential for getting out of that hole; but the potential needed motivation.

This story illustrates, if rather crudely, that resident in you, in me, and in every person is the potential for lifting ourselves up out of defeat. It just needs a force to be applied.

The quartermaster was making his routine rounds of the ship, when he suddenly noticed in the water, clearly revealed in the moonlight, a cylindrical black object. Aghast, he realized that it was a live contact mine that had broken loose from a mine field. It was slowly drifting in a direction that would bring it up against the destroyer amidship. The quartermaster seized the intercom and called the duty officer, who came dashing to the scene with the captain.

A general alarm was sounded, and the whole ship burst into action. In consternation, the officers and men viewed the mine that was approaching ever nearer to the ship. Quickly, they considered what could be done. Could they up anchor? No, they didn't have time. Could they start the engines and swing the ship around? No, because the propeller wash would only suck in the mine faster. Could they explode it by gunfire? No, that would not work because of the proximity to the ship's magazine. Could they launch a boat and push it away? That was ruled out, for it was a contact mine. Seemingly, there was nothing to do but to alert the officers and men to brace themselves for a terrible catastrophe.

However, among the men on deck was an ordinary seaman who outthought all his superiors. 'Get the fire hoses!' he cried. What a simple, practical idea. They played a stream of water between the ship and the mine so that it created a current that moved the mine out to a safe distance, where they destroyed it by gunfire.

Quite a man, that seaman, wouldn't you say? Now what was it that he had? First, it was clarity of mind. There was nothing confusing his thought processes. He was operating on all cylinders, so to speak. No tension or inner conflict inhibited his mental powers. As a result, he was able to think in a crisis, and he produced a creative solution to a tough problem.

The human mind is so constituted that if you pour your attention onto a problem without panic, keeping yourself calm and your mind unruffled, and if you maintain faith in God and firmly believe that you are going to get an answer, the answer will appear. Moreover, the more spiritual your mind is, the more definitely will it produce in this manner.

Use Creative Silence

The eminent US industrialist Robert G. LeTourneau, manufacturer of earthmoving machinery, once received a wartime order from the US government for a very complicated large machine to lift airplanes. No machine of the kind envisaged had ever been designed.

LeTourneau and his engineers went to work on the problem, but it baffled them. They worked at it for several days, but they weren't getting anywhere. They all became tense and nervous. Finally, as Wednesday night came around, LeTourneau said, 'Well, boys, I'm knocking off. I'm going to a prayer meeting.'

'Why,' they said, 'you can't do that, boss. We've got a deadline on this thing.'

'But,' he said, 'I've got a deadline with God.' He went to prayer meeting, dropping the problem into the deep well of his unconscious mind. He sang hymns, and he prayed. He got himself into harmony with God. What happened after the meeting? LeTourneau reported that as he was walking along the street, there in his mind, in complete detail, was the design of the machine. It had been there all the while, of course, and he needed creative silence to bring it forth.

What is your problem? Is it one of health, of business, of your children, of your future? It makes no difference what it is. Do not get agitated, nor depressed over it. Do not try so hard. Do not be in a panic. Do not overstress it. Whatever your problem, when you lift your spirits, clear your mind, believe in your potential, take the worry and fear out of your thoughts, and have faith in God, you can do the impossible. You surely can.

As long as you are alive, you can do something about your problems.

Chapter 3

You can overcome any problem

Courage is fear
that has said its prayers.

𝒫roblems are never in short supply. But today they seem accentuated both in number and intensity. An old spiritual says 'nobody knows the trouble I've seen.' Similarly, we often feel that nobody suffers the difficulties that throng about us and harass us.

This chapter is designed to offer suggestions not merely to help you meet and endure difficulties. It's much more than that. It is an action plan. And its purpose is to show you how to overcome your problems... and overcome them now. It's an overcome now formula.

A young man whom I once met in an airport told me: 'I've got plenty of problems. But don't do any worrying about me. God and I together can handle all difficulties. Be seeing you.' And he walked off jauntily! It was evident that he had the components of the answer. He was thinking right; he faced his problems, and he had God going with him. And, I may add, so have you.

This chapter outlines a series of steps together with specific techniques that will work when worked, and with these you can make real progress in overcoming your problems. That is, if you will start, continue and not lose patience in the process. There will, of course, be times of discouragement, times when it seems no progress is being made. But keep thinking positively, stay with the effort and follow the suggestions given. I am sure you will overcome your problems because others have done so by following the action formulas suggested here.

Think Positively — Not Emotionally

At the very beginning of your effort to overcome your problems it will be necessary to take a positive mental attitude toward them, to think and believe that you can master them and that indeed you are now proceeding to do so. Do this and the action has begun.

In my office is a sign someone made for me. It reads 'Attitudes are more important than facts.' That legend has proved helpful in handling my own problems because it teaches how to look at a fact. The negativist may say, 'Here is a hard, tough fact. You just can't get around a fact. A fact is a fact and that is that.'

But the positivist on the other hand says, 'Yes, it is a fact. That must be recognized. But there is a way to deal with this or any fact: go around it or under it or over it or hit it straight on. A fact is for solving and I've got what it takes to do just that.'

The negativist is likely to be defeated by the fact, while the positivist will probably handle it creatively. It is not so much the fact as your attitude toward the fact that determines the outcome.

How you think about a problem is the issue of paramount importance. You can think yourself to success, or you can think yourself to failure. You can think yourself to victory over your problems, or you can think yourself to defeat by them. The kind and manner of your thought determine the eventual results you will experience.

The Law of Attraction

There is a law called the law of attraction. Like attracts like. 'Birds of a feather flock together.' Thoughts of a kind have a natural affinity. Therefore the negative thinker sending forth negative thoughts, stimulating the world around him negatively, draws back to himself, in the very nature of the case, negative results. That which you yourself send out in the way of thought is bound to come back to you.

The positive thinker on the other hand sends out of his brain positive, optimistic, faith-filled thoughts. He activates the world around him positively. On the basis of the same law of attraction he tends thereby to draw back to himself positive results.

Consider the case of two salesmen. One was assigned territory which had produced very little business for the company. This territory had the reputation that 'nobody can do anything with it.'

This man went to his new territory in full acceptance of the general appraisal that there was no business possibility there. 'So,' he reasoned, 'why knock myself out? I am being unfairly treated by having this non-producing area hung around my neck.' You will not be surprised to know that he failed to develop any appreciable amount of new business and left the company. He never even gave it a try. It was for him a fact that no opportunity was available there. His attitude toward it was negative. Results? Negative!

A second salesman, brought in from across the country, knew nothing about the territory except that it was centered around a thriving metropolitan community. No one had told him that it contained no sales possibility, so he proceeded to get busy and make many sales. 'Why, this is an unworked gold mine!' he exclaimed. All his thinking was positive and his activity was positive. He made a great success of the territory. But so profound was this man's positive mental attitude that had anyone told him it was a bad territory he wouldn't have believed it. And why should he? There were hundreds of thousands of people living there and they needed his product and he was there to see that they had it. He was a successful man.

You can think your way through and finally out of any difficulty or problem. But you must think, not react emotionally. When a difficulty strikes, the tendency is to panic or to be upset, even to be resentful. Such reactions are emotionally conditioned, and if one's acts are determined in such a state of mind they are likely to be lacking full rationality.

One must discipline himself to be calm in his thinking. He must cool it. For the mind cannot think when it is hot; only when the mind is cool will it produce those rational factual concepts which lead to solutions. So do not allow yourself to emote. Think!

Actually, your head is your greatest asset. Keep it always under disciplinary control. Remember the statement credited to Thomas A. Edison, 'The chief purpose of the body is to carry the brain around.' The great inventor knew that it is in the mind, working in non-overheated fashion, that we get ideas, not impulses. And with these sound ideas we solve problems.

Action Steps
1. Take positive mental attitude toward any problem.
2. Stop all negative thoughts, all negative talks.
3. Affirm that your attitude toward a fact is more important than the fact.
4. Emphasize the law of attraction. Attract by your positive thinking only positive results.
5. Discipline yourself to keep your mind always calm. Cool it.

Take Worry Apart!

Replace worry. Banish worry to let joy and happiness in. People can't quit worrying because they can't let go of ingrained ways of thinking. The way to break this pattern is to take hold of a good idea to enable yourself to let go of a bad one.

Take worry apart. Since worry is an irrational thought, you must take worry apart, lay it out, dissect it, cut up, and look at it piece by piece. Do this with cool, collected, rational thought. Worry is a deceiver, but once you face up to it squarely, you will be able to handle it.

Get the heat and emotion out of worry, and put cold, ruthless scrutiny onto the problem, and worry loses its power. When we are worried and filled with apprehension, we become panicky and are likely to see only gloom and failure. There isn't any situation so bad that it won't become a lot better when you think rationally — and spiritually — about it. God gives you the ability to think rationally about things by filling you with peace and faith.

Some years back, full of fret and worry over a problem, I talked to Dr. David Keppel, a wise and logical man. 'Norman,' he said, 'let us sit down and take this worry apart.' And remarkably, when he got through with it, there wasn't much left. He said that 90 percent of his own worries were never realised. 'And I was able to handle the ten pecent that was left.' Dr. Keppel wrote a poem about this process.

Better never trouble trouble
    until trouble troubles you,
For you're sure to make your trouble
    Double trouble when you do.
And your trouble, like a bubble,
    that you're troubling about,
May be nothing but a cipher
    With the rim rubbed out.

When you turn a hard eye onto a problem, worry will lose its power. There isn't any situation so bad that it won't become a lot better when you think rationally — and spiritually — about it. When you do, God will fill you with peace.

Rise above worry. Next time you find yourself bogged down in anxiety and worry, say to yourself, 'I will think this thing through. I will take it apart. I will not be disturbed by it.' If you practice this, worry will melt away.

Replace Worry

Worry has been described as a spasm of the emotions, a catalyst for creating a depressed condition within a human being. Banish worry and you will permit the positive emotions of joy and happiness to rise to the surface. Worry is a condition in which the mind spasmodically clutches an idea and won't let it go. That is the reason you are never successful in telling people to quit worrying. They can't quit worrying. Their minds are in an emotional spasm. They are holding onto some obsessive idea and can't let it go. The only way to break the spasm is to insinuate another idea into this spasmodic grip, until the mind lets go of the bad idea and seizes the good idea.

I talked with a woman whose doctor had told her there was nothing the matter with her, yet she insisted she didn't feel well and was depressed. She had suffered an attack two years before, one of those warning attacks that is often actually a good thing, since it warns you to take care of yourself. 'I know the doctors say there is nothing wrong with me, now,' she reiterated. 'But maybe it will come back.'

Her mind had that spasmodic grip on the idea that she would have another attack. She dwelled upon the idea so completely that her spirits spiralled down and she enjoyed no part of her life. I inserted the idea that God had spared her, because He wanted her to do a constructive job of service for Him. This idea of faith finally became embedded in her consciousness, and it presently broke the negative cycle that gripped her life.

Rise Above Worry

Worry is a peculiar thing. It is like a dust storm on a hot day. You can become confused and lose your way. I was in Kansas, when a death occurred in my family and I had to fly to Cincinnati. A friend sent me in a private plane. When we were crossing the Mississippi River, the sky grew hazy. 'We can't see where we're going.' I said to the pilot. He replied, 'We'll go up above the haze-level.'

'What's the haze-level?' I asked.

'Ground heat, dust, and smoke combine to form the haze-level,' he explained. 'We'll go up another thousand feet and get above it.' We did, and emerged into an altogether different world, one clear and beautiful. The pilot commented, 'Life is something like this, isn't it? Look at those people down there groping in the haze. Up here, we have clarity and can see our way.'

We must employ the message Almighty God has given us and get above the haze-level. Next time you

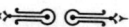

Most people don't plan to fail,
they fail to plan.

— *John L. Beckley*

find yourself bogged down in anxiety and worry, say to yourself, 'I will think this thing through. I will take it apart. I will not be disturbed by it. I will rise above the haze-level.' If you practice this, you willl find that your worry has lost its power.

Replace Fear With Action

Normal fear is necessary for our protection. But abnormal fear is altogether different. Sad indeed are people who walk in the terror of abnormal fear. It causes depression and anxiety — even physical illness.

The only fear we should have is the fear of God and the fear of doing wrong. That is not fear in the sense of being scared; rather, it is a respect of God and of what is right. We should walk unafraid.

Believe in Yourself. You may say: I am tired of being afraid of illness and of other people and of possible catastrophes. I want to be free of fear always. If so, the first thing you must realize about fear is that most of what you are afraid of probably will never happen.

One absolute way to let go of fear is to practice prayer by affirmation: not the prayer of asking, but the prayer of affirming. Believe the God loves you and that He watches over you. Believe He is taking care of you right now and that you need not be afraid. Do not say, 'O Lord, please deliver me from fear. I am so tired of being upset.' Rather, affirm that He is already doing it, and you will drop fear.

Stand up to fear. Fear can't be evaded or avoided. It has to be met head on. If you don't go to the heart of your fear, that fear will haunt you.

Action is the only answer.

Fear of trying something new is normal. When a child enters a new school, or when someone starts a new job, there is fear. But if he or she acts with confidence and faith, fears vanish. And a glowing sense of accomplishment comes with trying something new and succeeding.

Let fear motivate you. Every person has the potential for overcoming defeat. Faith in God is a mighty force that you can call on to make your life count. Faith in God and in yourself can rid you of fear forever.

Don't Be An 'If' Thinker, Be A 'How' Thinker

When J. C. Penney, the famous merchant and a longtime friend of mine, was a vigorous 95 years old, we were seated together at the speaker's table in the Grand Ballroom of the Hotel Waldorf-Astoria in New York. We fell to discussing problems and what to do about them. 'You have had plenty of difficulty in your long lifetime, J.C.,' I said. 'What is your philosophy of a problem?'

His answer was characteristic of this great and good man. 'Well, Norman,' he replied, 'actually I'm grateful for all my problems. As each of them was overcome I became stronger and more able to meet those yet to come. I grew on my difficulties.'

Believe you can and you can — this dynamic principle has been demonstrated in the lives of too many believers to leave any doubt concerning its validity. It is very important to believe that you can, with God's help, meet and overcome all problems. And the more profoundly you believe, the more surely you will gain victory. The words *believe* and *can* are linked together in a creative action unity. If you believe you can, you can.

Let me tell you about Fred Haas, one of those rare believers who is made by all-out faith. He believed his way gloriously through a mass of problems.

After 30 years of hard work Fred lost his business because of a crooked partner. I expected him to be full of bitterness when he came to see me. Instead, he told me that he had found his assests to be much greater than his liabilities.

'All I had when I began thirty years ago was $50. Now I have $500, so, you see, I'm ahead on that,' he said with a grin. 'I started with a wonderful wife, and I still have her, thank God. And I'm way ahead on experience.'

Within a year after this setback he had got another business started and was doing well. But the statement he made which really stayed with me was this: 'I decided I would not be an *if* thinker, but a *how* thinker.'

That's really quite a thought-provoking distinction. The *if* thinker broods over a difficulty or a setback, saying bitterly to himself, 'If only I had done thus and so ... If only this or that circumstance had been different ... If others had not treated me so unfairly ...' So it goes from explanation to explanation, round and round, getting nowhere. The world is full of defeated *if* thinkers.

The *how* thinker, on the other hand, wastes no energy on post-mortems when trouble or even disaster hits him, but immediately starts looking for the best solution, for he knows there always is a solution. He asks himself, 'How can I use this setback creatively? How can I work something good out of it?'

The *how* thinker gets problems solved effectively because he knows that values are always inherent in difficulty. He wastes no time with futile *ifs* but goes right to work on the creative *how*.

The next time trouble strikes you, avoid the word *if*. Focus on the dynamic word *how*. Then ask God's help to put know-how into the how. You will be amazed at how quickly your problems will be resolved.

'Problems toughen my mind'

Charles F. Kettering, famous research scientist, was a wise man, a kind of natural-born philosopher. He was an inventive genius of high order, especially in the automotive field.

I had a most illuminating conversation with this great thinker in the course of which he expounded his philosophy on problems. 'I could do nothing without problems' he declared emphatically, 'they toughen my mind. In fact,' he said, 'I tell my assistants not to bring me their successes, for they weaken me; but rather to bring me problems, for they strengthen me.'

One reason the believer successfully believes his way through problems is that he never runs away. He is not so superficial and foolish as to think that if he can just run out on his present difficulties things will be easier elsewhere. He knows that the same or similar difficulties will follow him wherever he goes, and that the only sure way to stop running is to stand up to those problems right where he is and fight the battle. And this applies to all of us. If you do not defeat problems right here and right now, they will chase and hound you the rest of your life. Don't run; fight it out, believe it through — now, and right where you are. That is the formula that works with that phenomenon called a problem.

I met a young man who positively exuded dynamic confidence. He was in sales and it was evident that he was literally bursting with enthusiasm for his job and for salesmanship generally. 'I love to sell,' he declared. 'I just love it. There is nothing like the challenge and excitement of selling.' He was most impressive and inspirational.

But he admitted that he had not always had this positive mental attitude and undefeatable spirit. Far from it. Formerly he was afraid to call upon a potential buyer. To make a 'cold' call practically terrified him. So overwhelmed was he that he would lie on a couch in his home afraid to go out to do his job. He alternately went hot and cold and literally cowered with fear. He was completely defeated. And yet, really he wasn't because he continued to think and pray. As a result, an idea came which saved him.

Being very personable, he was offered a job by another organization — a job much easier than his selling job. He was delighted and terribly relieved. Even at the start, this new job would net him twice the amount he was currently making. What a wonderful out. He could escape this sales job which frightened him so much.

But the idea that saved him from making a mistake, the idea that came through thinking and praying, was that running never got you anywhere except into more running. If he did not win the battle with fear right where he was, fear would follow him wherever he went, however inviting a new job seemed.

So he asked the Lord's help. He stood up to his fears. He refused to run. He declined the attractive job opportunity. He decided he would 'fight the good fight, finish the course, and keep the faith.' God gave him the strength that He always gives to anyone who believes. The young man conquered his fears. He not only learned to sell, he learned to love it. And a few years later the company whose job offer he had declined offered him an even better position.

So, never run from difficulties. Believe your way through them. And you can if you believe you can. God is always standing with you, and His help never fails.

Action Steps

1. Believe in God.
2. Believe in yourself.
3. Grow strong on your problems.

4. Believe you can and you can.
5. Saturate your mind with faith.
6. Don't be an *if* thinker. Be a *how* thinker.
7. Never run from a problem — stand up to it.

Learn Know-How From Your Problems

Don't fight a problem. And never complain when a problem strikes you. Instead, start asking questions of the problem. For it is full of know-how for you. Actually, a problem is one of God's greatest methods for teaching you, for helping you to develop.

When a problem comes along, instead of bewailing and complaining, just say to God, 'Lord, what are you trying to teach me by this problem? What insights do You wish to give me?' Then tackle the problem, using all your thought power and prayer power. Some of the most amazing guidance you will ever experience will come to you as you crack open a problem. You will then have the know-how to overcome it.

People sometimes ask, 'Why must we have so many problems? Wouldn't life be simply wonderful,' they say, 'if we had fewer problems or easier problems or, better still, no problems at all?' This attitude is based on the widely held assumption that there is something inherently bad about a problem. But, on the contrary, may it not be true that a problem can be a very good thing? May it not be filled with possibility and potential?

Would you actually be better off if you had fewer problems, or easier problems or no problems whatsoever?

The answer is that those who have no problems are in the cemetery. For them life's fitful fever is over; they rest from their labours. They couldn't care less about all that goes on in this life. They have no problems at all; but they are dead. It follows therefore in logical sequence that problems constitute a sign of life. Indeed, the more problems you have, the more alive you are.

So, rather than complaining, be glad that you have problems, for it means you are alive and vital and that God believes you possess the ability to handle problems.

Look at every problem as containing some amazing value for you. When God wants to give you something of great worth, does He present it on silver plater as something that comes easy? Not often. He is more likely to bury it at the core of a tough, hard problem.

That precious value may be difficult to come by but if you view every problem as a value container rather than something to harass you, the result will be greater knowledge and achievement than ever before.

If you approach a problem spiritually with full mental effort and then add a genuine faith, insights and guidance will be given to you amazingly. You may actually receive specific direction. God will show you what to do about your problem. You will be given great power over it. But how can you know what steps to take, what decisions to make, which way to turn? There are several ways, but one is the method of the 'closed doors.'

My mother used to tell me, 'When a door slams shut in your face it's just God guiding you.' I personally found that belief in this principle and long-time application of it gave me victory over disappointment and apparent defeat. I went forward confidently toward the open door.

So be grateful for your problems. They are full of values for you, if you believe.

Action Steps

1. Don't fight a problem. Always ask questions of it. Ask, 'What is God saying to me in this problem?'
2. Be glad you have problems for it proves you are alive.
3. Believe that a problem is not inherently bad but good.
4. See buried in every problem an amazing value for you.
5. Approach every problem with a think-pray-believe formula.
6. Go forward on the amazing closed-door, open-door technique.

You Are Bigger Than Your Problem

In the process of overcoming any problem it is important to have a proper appraisal of yourself in relation to the problem. And the truth we want to emphasize with all force and sincerity is that you are bigger than your problem. And that goes for any issue you will ever be called upon to face. So now affirm strongly and believe it: 'I am bigger than any problem. I can overcome any

So You've Got a Problem, Congratulations!

Some years ago I knew an inspirational man who taught me the technique of looking for 'the pearl of great price' buried at the heart of a problem. As a young man burdened by a seemingly insoluble problem I went to him for advice. 'So you've got a problem,' he said. 'Congratulations!'

'Why congratulations?' I asked in surprise. Sympathy seemed more in order. 'Because,' he replied cheerfully, 'out of this problem some big wonderful thing may come into your life.'

At his encouragement I outlined the problem in full detail. He listened carefully as I laid the entire problem out before him. 'There it is, this big problem of yours. Now what do we do? First let's not be afraid, certainly not be awed by it. The face of it is not grim. Actually it is smiling at you, asking that you play hide and seek with it. There is something great hiding in it. The fun is for you to find it. Something God put there in that problem is for you and God gave you the brains to think it through and to find know-how within it.'

Whimsically he began poking with his forefinger at an imaginary mass laid on the table. 'Every problem has a soft spot,' he explained. 'We'll find it.' Presently he chuckled, 'Here it is. Now let's start breaking this problem apart. I'm sure we will find something wonderful in it.' And under his skillful guidance we did find one of the greatest value in my personal experience. I have had profound respect for problems. Ever since, knowing that each one that comes my way may come bearing a priceless gift of know-how, insight and understanding.

problem.' Do not doubt, for your affirmation is sound and true.

The basis for this confidence in yourself is that you are a child of God, created in the Divine Image. No group of factors can match such a relationship: When God made you He made you great. He made you strong. Practice believing this until you accept it fully in the depths of consciousness and you will presently come to know for certain that you are bigger than your problem.

Our tendency often is to feel inferior and inadequate in the presence of a problem. We may even be obsessed with a haunting, conflicted sense of our inability to cope with the problems of human existence generally, and with the present problem in particular. In the mind one tends to blow the problem up in imagination to an extent that is out of all proportions to its actual size. It scares and frightens not because it is too big for us but because our fearful thoughts have invested it with a difficulty that it does not really possess.

An important procedure then is to cut the problem down to its true proportions; reduce it to size. Empty out the fear-panic-inadequacy feeling and start thinking with objective rationality. See the problem straight. Defuse emotional reactions. Activate creative thought.

In a business office I found a man behind a desk on which sheets of paper all of a size were laid out in orderly pattern. Each sheet contained handwritten notations. This man said, 'You may be curious about what goes on here with these papers. Actually I'm dealing with a pretty big and rough problem. And I have my own way of doing that.'

He went on to tell me that there was a time in his life when he was 'licked' by a problem and, in fact, was dismayed when he was called upon to face one. Usually the problem seemed overwhelming. Then he met an older businessman who said, 'Look, Jack, I've found that usually no problem is as forbidding as it seems. I discovered that if you begin taking a problem apart, breaking it up into its component parts you can handle the whole problem by dealing with those parts separately. Take a problem in bits and pieces. You can handle them by that method. And the bits and pieces will add up to handling the entire problem. Try this way and the matter won't look so big to you.'

'That advice made sense,' my friend said, 'so my method is what you see here. I thoroughly analyze the problem, breaking it up and writing on these papers its various aspects. Then,' he continued, 'I pray and ask for guidance as to how to proceed. Usually I gain an insight from the prayer, as a result of which I select one element of the problem with which to begin.

'I 'chisel' off the easiest part first and dispose of that. In this manner I continue to work and pray until the problem is reduced to its central core. Then it's wonderful how adequate I feel in dealing with the essence of the matter. This method really work,' he declared enthusiastically, 'so much so that I'm getting a greater kick out of life than ever. I've found that I am bigger than any problem,' he concluded stoutly.

So never let any problem overawe you. You are bigger than it is. You have the mental and spiritual power to overcome it. Take the problem calmly and confidently as it comes. Never depreciate yourself or emphasize your limitations. Many defeated persons are defeated simply because they are 'self-limitators.' Their self-image causes them to see themselves as weak and incompetent. You are what your self-image is. So begin changing your self-image. Cast off the self-limiting concepts which are rendering you ineffective. Be what you really are —, a child of God, unlimited, free and great, really great. Start being that now in your mind and presently you will be that in fact.

Never Build a Case Against Yourself

One of the greatest gems of wisdom ever given to me was a statement by a lifelong friend, Rob Rowbottom. A man of strong faith, a true child of God, he said, 'Never build a case against yourself.' So utterly right, so profoundly powerful is that insight that you would do well to write it on a card. Carry it in your wallet. Paste it on your mirror. Slip it under the glass top of your desk. Tack it above the kitchen sink. But better still, imprint it in consciousness until it really takes hold and starts motivating you. It's simply terrific! It's wonder-working! 'Never build a case against yourself.'

And what does it mean? Simply this: That no longer are you going to tell yourself what you can't do, that you are an inferior person lacking in ability, not capable of overcoming your problems. From now on you are striking the 't' off that word 'can't' so that it stands out clear and strong, 'I can because I am.' Am what? A child of God, one who is intended not to be defeated by life but to master it.

~

Turn your former self-limiting concepts into self creating factors. Like Tom Dempsey, for example.

The sports pages told of this remarkable football player, Tom Dempsey of the New Orleans Saints, who single-handedly won a game over the New York Giants. He was considered by some to be the greatest field-goal kicker in the game. With unerring accuracy he booted the ball right over the crossbar. He once kicked a record 63-yard field goal, breaking the previous record by 7 yards. He was a genius with the foot — and that is because he was also a genius with the mind.

His foot was motivated by a positive mental attitude, for Tom Dempsey was born with a half-formed right foot. He had to wear an orthopeadic kicking shoe that cost him $200. But with that half foot he made stellar kicks.

And that isn't all of it. Tom Dempsey was born with a right hand that had no fingers. Now how in the world are you going to hold a ball with a hand that has no fingers and drop it properly to a half foot? The way you do it is to believe that you can do it! One sportswriter asked him, 'How do you do so well being handicapped?'

He replied, 'I don't know that word. I never thought of myself as being handicapped. And as for the word *can't* it doesn't exist in my vocabulary.'

Don't let it exist in your vocabulary, either. You are bigger than your problem, and that goes for whatever your problem may be.

Action Steps

1. Get a right appraisal of yourself in relation to your problem.
2. Affirm and do not doubt. 'I can overcome any problem because I'm bigger than it is.'
3. Every day say, 'I am a child of God.'
4. Cut every problem down to size. Chip off the easiest elements first until you can handle the problem's core.
5. Never let any problem overawe you.
6. Do not depreciate yourself. Impose no self-limitations.
7. Never build a case against yourself.
8. Build up your self-image.
9. Throw the word 'can't' out of your vocabulary.

All resources we need are in
the mind.

— *Theodore Roosevelt*

God Is With You

When we assert that you can overcome any problem, we are taking into account that you do not have to do it entirely on your own. For, you see, God is with you. You have His big extra help available. Thus, you have the advantage of insight and strength greater than any human being possesses. What problem can possibly be too much for God and you acting together in perfect harmony? It's the greatest combination of all.

And how can you be sure that God is with you personally — and very near, at that? One method is to practice God's presence. Talk with Him in the mind, think with Him. Try to act like Him, making every effort to conduct yourself as you believe God wants you to live. Constantly employ the assumption that God is at your side, indeed even nearer than that. He is within your very nature. In due course the assumption will give way to certainty of the fact. You will know without any doubt whatsoever that the presence is real, completely valid.

A man consulted me once who dismally complained that he was overwhelmed by problems and couldn't see his way through them. Knowing this man quite well, I was aware of the quality of his mind. While at the moment his thoughts were under a heavy cover of dark clouds, I was sure that he possessed the capacity to believe. I had confidence that he would be able to believe his way out of this gloomy mental overcast.

My suggestion to him was that he practice the presence of God in every way possible. He was to talk to God as he drove his car. Walking along the street, he was to affirm that God actually walked with him. In a restaurant, if he could unobtrusively do so, he was to pull alongside an empty chair by his bed. The objective was to effect, through such practice, a mental attitude that would develop faith far greater than his problems.

I must say that this man really went all out in objectifying the Divine Presence. It became an integral part of his daily routine, so much so that one night, walking out of sleep, he placed his hand on the nearby chair and actually 'felt' that his hand was grasped.

'Of course, my mind could have been playing tricks on me,' he said. 'But I don't believe it. I know for a fact that He was there by my bed. And I can tell you why I'm so certain. It's because now those problems no longer lick me at all. I'm on top of them. I know that God is with me because things go easier. And those dark clouds have lifted off my mind.'

So the suggested action is to practice the Presence in whatever way may seem most meaningful. This practical activation of faith, this objectifying of belief, manifests itself in a convincing actuality of God as with you, helping you. And with it you are equal to any problem. Try it and discover this great fact for yourself. Get with it. Get with God.

Often it has been demonstrated that the thought of God activates forces which so completely revolutionize persons that problems which formerly defeated them are overcome by the power of the God thought. This thought of God has shown itself able to cut through a mass of defeat attitudes and let in the clear and healing light of truth.

Take the well-known singer, Johnny Cash, as an example of this process. According to a magazine article, he woke up one morning in jail. He was not there for any misdemeanor, but for his own protection. He had been on pills, 'looking for peace.' He admits that he became afraid of everything. Before a performance he was a nervous wreck, sometimes almost too sick to work. Sometimes he did not even appear for a scheduled show. Now here he was lying on a jail cot staring at the ceiling.

'I'm a fan of yours, Johnny,' said the elderly jailer. 'It's a shame to see you ruining yourself. I didn't know you were this bad off.' As he opened the door for the singer the old man continued, 'Your great talent came from God. You're sure wrecking the body He put it in.'

As Cash stepped into the warm sunshine the word 'God,' dropped by the jail keeper, kept reverberating through his mind. Until then it had never occurred to him that God could or would help him with his problem or give him the strength to kick his habit. He realized that to be free he would have to have help. 'I asked God to go to work on me right then and there,' he said later. Needless to say, he fought the battle and won. He found that with God he could overcome his problem.

Johnny Cash's experience gives us a real action formula. 'Let God go to work on you.' He will work you over until you can handle any problem no matter how tough it may be. Think God. Think God. Think God. And then let Him do the work in you. He will.

Still another procedure is to believe in God in depth and to nourish that belief until you learn to trust. Belief is intellectually based. It involves acceptance of the truth of God in one's thinking. Trust may be defined as belief activated. In this instance you rest completely and wholly on your faith, trusting it to sustain you and see you through whatever, wherever, and whenever the crisis. When you feel inadequate to meet and deal with a problem that seems overwhelming, the practice of trust in God bring to your aid immense and unsuspected resources.

Action Steps

1. Practice the presence of God.
2. Work on developing your capacity to believe.
3. Believe your way out of a mental overcast. Faith dissipates gloominess.
4. Objectify the Divine Presence. Practice His reality.
5. Believe and affirm that, since God is for you, nothing can be against you.
6. Make use of the powerful God thought.
7. Practice trust until you can trust. Then trust.

The Think-pray Formula

To handle any problem successfully, pray your way over it. This is the surest and safest way to overcome any problem.

It is safe and sure, for it draws upon insight and wisdom that is bound to be superior to your own, involving as it does the guidance of the greatest mind of all.

Utilize the think-pray formula. Human intelligence plus Divine intelligence is more than sufficient to handle successfully any problem you will ever be called upon to face in life. What you can't think of, God can. The answers that you do not know, He does.

A procedure which many have found effective is to sit down and carefully write out your problem in detail. You will know more certainly exactly what you have to deal with. And more than likely as you write it out you will at once begin to see new lines of approach hitherto obscured. As a result there will begin to come to you the happy feeling that you can, after all, overcome this problem.

Seeing it more definitively, you can now proceed to make it come out as it should. Writing makes for organization, for unravelling and clarification. Reduce the problem to its simplest one, two, threes and then the steps leading to solution will start falling in place.

Having written the problem out in the detailed manner described, the next step in the process of solution is to attack the situation with prayer. And that prayer must of course be more than a kind of frantic, 'God help me!' appeal. Indeed if the frantic element is involved it can frustrate the cool rational thinking by which anything is thought through. The secret is to employ prayer in depth, this kind of prayer requires discipline and sustained effort.

Let me tell you about a young man who became literally a genius in getting right solutions to problems. From a floundering person, defeated most of the time, he developed into an extraordinarily competent individual. To his problems he got answers that really answered. The method he evolved was amazing in the high score he attained in right solutions.

His method consisted, first, of writing the problem in meticulous detail. Then he studied what he had written, and in instances where he lacked familiarity with some particular factor he would assiduously research it. 'You can't think in the dark. You've got to know all you can about everything involved,' he explained. 'Otherwise you may miss the point of the whole thing.'

Having done his own mental homework, he was now ready 'to get a real mind going' for him, to use his own words. 'I had evolved my own ideas by now, as to the

'I Don't Believe in Circumstances'

The glib idea of 'circumstances beyond our control' is too often used to rationalize a feeble giving up too soon.

'I don't believe in circumstances,' said George Bernard Shaw. 'The people who get on in this world are the people who get up and look for the circumstances they want, and, if they can't find them, make them.'

That is the attitude that works wonders in problems.

steps to take and the decisions to make. But since I'm a human being I can think wrong, very wrong, and make stupid choices. Therefore, I now set about getting the Lord's ideas and decisions.' This conditioned the mind to be receptive to God's suggestions and got him into spiritual harmony so that the guidance insights could come through.

He would then 'tell the Lord' of his own desires, the kinds of answers he would like and the solution as it appeared to him. But then he would add, 'But if what I want isn't good and if my solutions are off the beam, please make me willing to accept, instead, what you want for me. And please brief me on Your decisions. I want to do it Your way.'

Following this mental and spiritual conditioning, the young man then practiced what he called a 'quiet time,' body relaxed, mind unhurried and peaceful. The agitated and ruffled-up mind can often prevent insights from arising out of the deeper levels of consciousness. Accordingly, it is of the utmost importance to cultivate, by meditation, relaxed, quiescent state to open up lines of spiritual communication.

Now I want to re-stress something mentioned in an earlier section, though differently applied. It is the positive-thinking-prayer approach to a problem. Add to this the sincere effort to do all that you possibly can about a problem situation. Then, having done all ... stand. Let go and let God. It will then work out as it should, which means as He wants it to be.

But for our human part of the action a further ingredient is required. That ingredient is persistence. Never give up. Keep going, whatever the adversities. Face the problem calmly and intelligently. Examine the circumstances and do everything you can think to do about it. And never give up either in your thoughts or in your actions. Pray and believe and bring positive thinking to bear upon the situation. *And never give up.*

When everything seems to be going wrong, you have a great opportunity for practicing the positive mental prayer attitude, believing that with God's help you can achieve your objective. If you think something is hopeless, your state of mind will actually attract further trouble to defeat you. Hold the thought that conditions will shift in your favour — and get going.

Action Steps

1. Pray your way over your problem — pray confidently.
2. Utilize the think-pray formula.
3. Write out your problem in detail to externalize the problem, rather than allow it to bog down in your mind.
4. Be sure to reduce the human error element by emphasizing God's truth.
5. Practice the quiet time to get the mind quiescent, thus allowing intuitions from deeper levels to float to the surface.
6. Do all that you can, then leave the results to God. Let go and let God.

7. Practice mental and spiritual thought conditioning.
8. Never give up, never — always keep going for right solutions.

There Is a Solution To Every Problem

Never will you have a problem so great that it cannot be overcome. Just keep that fact in mind. Of course, this is not to say that you will have only easy problems. Indeed you may have some that are incredibly difficult, great big problems that may seem completely overwhelming. But by your ability to think and pray and endure and strive and believe — you can overcome any problem life brings.

Never say that anything is hopeless. As someone once pointed out, 'There are no hopeless situations, only hopeless people.' Under no circumstances let yourself become so discouraged and negative as to give in to the feeling that you cannot see your way through a problem. Never, never, never give up, as Churchill once advised. Only those who give up are defeated by problems. The Lord has made this world so that man has the capacity to meet and think through and pray through any problem no matter how tough or complex it may be. Man has been given inner powers over his problems.

One of the power given to you is that of being able to 'hear,' by the deep inward ear which connects with your basic consciousness, the voice of God guiding you. Get attuned by thought and prayer and profound meditation and you can draw so near to God that His guidance will definitely come through. And especially is this true in crisis when suddenly great need is thrust upon you for the handling of which you feel totally incompetent. It is then that you will discover that all the time you have possessed an inner capacity that draws greater power to your aid.

For example, consider the story of Beth Black. One clear star studded night Mrs. Black was the sole passenger in a small plane piloted by her husband. They were over Dallas, Texas, and enjoyed the lights strung like necklaces over the terrain below.

Suddenly Mr. Black gasped and slumped dead in his seat of heart attack. Frozen with grief and terror, Mrs. Black was desperate. At first she thought of letting the plane crash so that she could die with her husband. But the thought of their young children at home deterred her.

She knew nothing at all about flying except that if you turned the wheel right or left the plane would bank in those directions and if you pushed the wheel forward the plane would nose down. If you pulled it back the aircraft would rise. But she was beside herself with panic. The gauges on the instrument panel were an incomprehensible jumble. She knew if she were to have any chance at all to survive she would have to get through to the control tower to receive guidance. She picked up the radio microphone. Frantically she cried into the various frequencies, 'Help. Someone. Oh, God please help me.' It was a desperate and urgent prayer.

And the prayer was being answered. Even this desperate problem was proving possible to overcome.

For amidst the static came a clear voice from the airport tower. Finally the voice got through her fears, guiding her step by step to an incredible, but safe landing. This woman, who had never flown a plane, who had watched aghast as her husband died, found astonishingly that she possessed an inner power hitherto unrealized.

Who can say that behind the human voice in the control tower is not a greater voice in a bigger control tower guiding all who trust to a solution to every problem? Flying blind in life as we often do, we can still listen for that voice. It will release power in you. Then you will know that every problem has its solution to which you will be guided.

Mr. W. Clement Stone has a fantastic attitude toward problems. I telephoned him at his Chicago office relative to a matter in which we were both interested. 'We have a problem,' I declared.

'That's wonderful!' he shouted back. 'That's good, a problem is always good. It means we may find better ways of doing things. And always remember, to every disadvantage there is an advantage.' Mr. Stone, who has spent his entire life taking problems apart, believes without question that every problem has its solution and that anyone can find it who really believes that he can.

Every Problem Contains the Seeds of its own Solution

Another friend, Stanley Arnold, came up with a phrase that deserves to be a classic. 'Every problem contains the seeds of its own solution.' The secret of problem solving is to look for those seeds. Some of which may be very small, but can lead to the center of the problem itself. Work with what you know about a problem, follow each factor back to its connection with the main matter at issue.

A businessman consulted me. He was very discouraged about a problem connected with his company. Having been for some days unable to find an answer, he was now on the verge of panic, so much so that his mind had frozen and was no longer operative. Certainly it was not delivering the necessary ideas.

He outlined the problem in detail. I encouraged him to talk and gave him plenty of time, in the hope that he might, as sometimes is the case, talk himself into a solution. But it did not work that way. Indeed the more he talked and wrestled with the problem the more his tension increased effectively closing off any possible creative thought. 'There just is no solution to this one,' he said dejectedly. 'I'm completely licked.'

'Oh, no, you are not,' I replied. 'And there is a solution to this problem. I'm sure of that because I've never yet seen a problem without a solution. Problems and solutions inevitably go together. You cannot have one without the other being right there all the time.'

I then suggested the mental defusing method by which the tension is broken by turning away from the problem. 'Let's forget it for a little while,' I suggested. 'Set it aside and for ten minutes or so let us think about God instead.

The man asked how you thought about God. And we discussed this totally different type of thought for a few minutes. All of this served to start a mental reconditioning and quieting of the mind. Then, stopping the discussion, I said, 'We will sit here quietly and think about God. I instructed my secretary not to interrupt us and for at least ten minutes the two of us sent our thoughts Godward. I knew it was being effective, for the atmosphere seemed actually to deepen, taking on an unmistakable spiritual sensitivity.

Finally he broke the silence. 'This is the first time I have felt relaxed and peaceful in days. I actually feel' — he searched for a word '— refreshed. That's it! I feel refreshed. I'm really untensed. What did you call it — "mental defusing?" Well, it works. I'm defused.'

He arose to leave. 'Thanks a lot,' he said. At the door he turned. 'What do you know? That's funny,' he mused, more to himself than to me. 'Why that's it. Of course it is. Why haven't I thought of it before?'

'Meaning what?' I asked.

'Meaning that I've got the beginning of the solution of my problem. You're right. You're so right,' he said. 'Indeed there is a solution to every problem.' Bypassing the problem through spiritual meditation defused him and permitted the solution to float to the surface of his mind. He discovered you can overcome any problem. So keep on believing, thinking, praying.

Action Steps

1. Believe there is a solution to every problem. Erase all doubts.
2. Never give up trying for the solution. Any problem will yield ultimately to sustained effort.
3. Affirm your capacity to solve your problem.
4. Cultivate the power to 'hear' by the inward ear and thus receive God's guidance.
5. Remind yourself that every disadvantage has a corresponding advantage.
6. Never forget that every problem contains the seeds of its own solution.
7. Practice meditation and experience mental defusing.
8. Keep on believing, thinking, praying.

Steps in Problem-Solving

Try these eight guidelines with your problem:

1. Don't panic. Keep calm. Use your head. You'll need all your wits.
2. Don't be overwhelmed by your problem. Don't get dramatic about it. Just tell yourself confidently, 'God and I can handle it.'
3. Practice de-confusion. A problem generally becomes surrounded by confusion. So de-confuse it. Write down every facet of the problem.

4. Ship the post-mortems. Don't ask, 'Why did I do that? Why didn't I do this' take the problem from where you now are.

5. Look for a solution, not for the whole problem, but for the next step.

6. Practice creative listening — to others through your other ear, and to God through your deep inner ear.

7. Always ask yourself what is the right thing to do in a given situation. Nothing wrong ever turned out right.

8. Keep praying. Keep thinking. Keep believing. And keep enthusiasm going, for it works miracles in problems.

Chapter 4

Positive change
for success

Be bold,
and mighty forces will
come to your aid.

I want to ask you a very personal, but very serious, question. Do you honestly believe you have a solid confidence in yourself? If you can answer yes with conviction, you have one of the greatest blessings you can get in this world. If you can't, then I can help you!

Since God created you, it is a given that he has confidence in you. It has been my experience that people do not break down because they are defeated, but because they *think* they are. They do not believe in their own possibilities. You need to trust in the abilities that God has given you.

Why shouldn't you believe in yourself? You are child of God; therefore, you have within you the great powers of God. Remember God's promise that he will never leave you alone or forget you. When you truly believe this, you are on your way to confident living. You do not have to fight your battles alone. God is at your side. He will stand by you and protect you for all of your life.

Possibility Thinking

Have you ever noticed how it is that so many of the greatest among us have risen from disadvantaged circumstances? There is one trait they all share; they are possibility thinkers. Not one of them said, 'I'm afraid I'll never make it' or 'I haven't got what it takes.' Thoughts like these are dangerous. If you go along telling yourself that you are a worm, your subconscious is going to believe it after a while. Your subconscious is very accommodating. It will send up to you exactly what you send down to it.

Never mind your circumstances. Listen to these lines from the poet, William Wordsworth:

> Trailing clouds of glory
>   do we come from God,
> who is our home.
> — *William Wordsworth*

This means *you*! You are a child of God, and there is greatness within you. You can be confident that the Lord is the strength of your life. Dare to be what God created you to be. Dare to be what you dream to be. Dare to be the finest you can be. God is your Father, and he has great hopes for you.

Plant in your mind pictures of accomplishment, achievement and personal fulfillment. Fill your conversations with words of faith and optimism, until faith and positive thinking become a part of your life. Don't let your down-times get the better of you, for good-times will surely come. Surrender your discouragement to God and then surrender yourself to Him. Lose yourself to Him, become a part of Him. He is strength, and He believes in you. If you have His love in your heart, nothing can defeat you.

Harmony

There is no greater victory in life than when you know that you are more than equal to any difficulties that come your way. The philosopher William James said, 'Be not afraid of life. Believe that life is worth living, and your belief will help create the fact.' When you are in loving harmony with God, then uncertainty and self-doubt melt away.

How can you achieve this happy condition? By applying creative thinking to unpleasant or defeating circumstances. The first step is to *believe* that you have what it takes to change them. Then you must humbly surrender yourself to God, seeking His wisdom and guidance. Then you must work at the problem, sometimes through pain and suffering.

First believe, then surrender, then work. These three actions will combine dynamically to effect positive change.

Keeping Emotions Under Control Every Day

The controlled person is a powerful person. He who always keeps his head will get ahead. And that is more than a play on words. The number of people who ruin their lives through lack of emotional control is considerable. To keep your emotions under control, I suggest these four steps:

1. When you begin to emotionalize rather than to think, it is well to stop and ask yourself, 'What would God do?' Then sit quietly thinking: Just what would you may have to wait and keep listening. And it requires a sensitive spiritual ear. Then just go ahead and do what you think He would do.

2. Subject your emotions to the cold treatment. The most dangerous element in emotional reaction is mental heat. So bring down your personality temperature by the application of mental coolness. Do this by calmly asking, 'What is the sensible thing to do? What is the right thing? What will happen if I fly off the handle and say the sharp mean word? What will it get me? What will it do to my influence? Will it hurt others?' Visualize possible after-effects. Follow this procedure and you will never have to say, sadly, 'I wish I hadn't done that.'

3. Today, try seeing how long you can refrain from the sharp retort, the barbed remark, the mean comeback. Deliberately discipline your volatile reactions. Put a curb on your tongue, but even more importantly, curb the mental attitude of which the tongue is only an instrument. The more you succeed in leaving sharp things unsaid, the more grateful you are going to be for this suggestion. People can and often do destroy their happiness in life by their tongues. They shoot

off an unfortunate remark or write a sharp letter, and the evil is done. And the real victim is not the other person, but oneself. So remember what the ancient philosopher Seneca said, for it is a very wise remark: 'The cure for anger is delay.' Delay and forget. You will be glad that you did.

4. Practice a relaxed, urbane, easy-going attitude. Now and then, sit loosely in a chair as limply as possible. Imagine yourself a burlap bag filled with potatoes. Cut the string, allowing the potatoes to roll out. Be like the bag that remains. Lift your arms one at a time, letting them fall limply like a wet leaf on a log. What is more relaxed than a wet leaf on a log? Do the same with your legs and eyelids, too. Conceive of all your muscles as completely relaxed. Now say, 'All tension is subsiding, all anger is leaving me. I am at peace. I am

Lessons from the Stock Market

Have you ever thought that there might be a lesson in the stock market? When you have a moment, take a look at a long-term graph of the Dow Jones Industrial Average in a newspaper. Notice how it rises and dips, rises and dips, but especially take note of how, over time, it always rises.

So it is with your life. You are going to have setbacks and defeats; sometimes, like the stock market, you will have an extended 'dip' in your fortunes.

Do not let this defeat you.

in harmony with God, with the world, with myself.' Then move deliberately. Speak softly. Only tense, tied-up people get out of emotional control. Ask the Lord to relax you.

Practice these four step faithfully, and they will help you maintain emotional control every day.

Humility and Modesty

A good friend of mine asked that I talk to his son who was failing out of college. My friend prepared me for this conversation by saying, 'Young people today aren't like their parents.' Personally, I think that's often just as well! The young man proceeded to tell me at great length what was wrong with his teachers. I never heard of such a poor bunch of professors in all my life! Finally, I said, 'Bill, it seems to me the first thing you must do is get a little humility.' After we prayed about this, Bill looked at me and said, 'O.K.' I'm getting the message. The fault is all mine.' *All right,* I thought, *now we're getting started.* It is always a good beginning to stop blaming others for your failures. But Bill grew despondent. 'I have so many faults,' he moaned. I brought him a pad and pencil and told him to list on one sheet all his negatives and on another, all his positives. The second sheet would include all the qualities that represented him as he would like to be. When he got his lists done, I asked him to put the first one away. 'That's the old Bill,' I told him. Then I suggested he fold up the positive sheet, keep it handy and read it a dozen times a day.

A few years later, Bill graduated in the top three of his class and got a good job. He still carried the positive sheet in his pocket and consulted it to make sure he was measuring up. He kept the negative one in his desk and, gradually, was crossing out his faults as he overcame them. He said, 'Don't worry, I'm not going to get cocky. I know it was God who gave me the strength.' And so God had, but only after Bill had dismissed his negatives and concentrated on his positives.

Jesus was born in a stable for a reason. It was God's choice for his son to be a man of the people and to live modestly. Jesus was comfortable among all, but he chose ordinary people to help him deliver the Good News. And what was the central message of this Good News? Love.

There is an inevitable and marvellous connection between modesty and confidence. If you want to live confidently, be modest about your circumstances, no matter how high or low. For the content man 'does not brag and is not proud.' And God loves him.

Partnership

Many of us, unhappily, have not done a very good job with the original material God built into us. We see others who we think are more gifted, smarter, better looking or who have had better luck. We doubt our strength and abilities. Too often self-doubt prevents people from living abundantly.

If this is your condition, you can change it. Daily say to yourself: 'God is now, this very moment, leading me into confident living. He is turning my weaknesses into strength. He has faith in me.' See yourself as God sees you. Remember He has created you in his image. Every day picture yourself as a person created in God's image. Think of God and you as joint partners in reaching all the potential that He has already wired into you. Cultivate a sound, humble awareness of the qualities within yourself that make for strength and power. Since God believes in you as your Creator and acts as your full partner, how can you not succeed?

I am Going To Like People Today and Every Day

When you really make up your mind to like people, it becomes so much easier to do just that. And liking people and having them like you is very important not only to your happiness, but to your welfare and success in life as well. We live in a world of people, and what they think about us is much involved in how well we do with life. You must like people and have good personal relations if you are to have a good day every day.

So, let's begin to practice liking people. How? Try these steps:

1. Start the day with a prayer of thanks for all your human relationships. While dressing, say to yourself, 'I am going to like people today and enjoy every personal contact. I am going to like him and her, and this person and that person,' and continue to list everyone with whom you associate. Run over in your mind some of the persons you love best. Visualize

their faces, recall happy experiences with them, and thank God for them.

2. Now bring into your thoughts one or two individuals whom you find difficult to like. Then, deliberately practice liking them. The fact that this may be a challenge does not mean it should not be done. Hard disciplines are good for the soul. They develop spiritual 'muscle.' The more victories in liking people you experience, the stronger and happier you will be today and every day.

3. In the process of learning to like a person, after you have taken the first step of making up your mind to like him or her, list whatever likeable qualities you can see in him. Start adding them up. This will predispose you toward liking him even as adding up the negatives has previously disposed you against him. As you proceed on this affirmative basis, you will be amazed at the previously unrealized attractive qualities the other person possesses. In time, you might even attain the attitude of the late Will Rogers who said, 'I never met a man I didn't like.'

4. A next step is to say something good about the person you are trying to like, and say it as often and to as many people as possible. But be sure you are honest in so doing, and not merely engaging in a strategy to gain a personal benefit.

5. Try to get this problem person to do a favour for you, if possible. If you do not like a person, or he you, and you do something for him, it can even increase his

dislike, since it puts him under obligation to you. He may even regard your action as patronizing. But if you encourage him to do something for you, he will feel complimented despite himself, and his good opinion of you will increase to a degree, at least, for you have shown that you respect his ability. You have treated his ego with esteem, and we tend to like anyone who does that for us.

6. Deliberately practice sending out thoughts of goodwill, love and esteem, beaming them to the person you have not liked or who does not like you. There is a powerful transmission force in such directed thought done in the person's presence or even in absentia. No directly spoken words are necessary. This goodwill communicates itself and stimulates reciprocal goodwill responses from the other individual. Do this every day. At the same time, hold a mental picture of your friendly thought 'reaching' the other.

7. Never accept your tendency to dislike anyone. Develop a genuine distaste for unfriendliness as a guard against slipping into a state of hostility. Constantly drain off accumulated dislike. Be sure to do so regularly until it is all gone completely and for good.

8. Practice the great spiritual and practical technique of the Scriptures: 'Love your enemies, bless them that curse you, do good to them that hate you, and pray for them which despitefully use you, and persecute you.' Constant, sincere, loving prayer ultimately dissolves hate and ill will.

Four steps
to achievement:
plan purposefully,
prepare prayerfully,
proceed positively,
pursue persistently.

— *William A Ward*

One of the most likeable men I ever knew is an executive of a big company in the Midwest. He likes everyone and everyone, it seems, likes him. I asked him how this liking attitude of his had developed. 'Well,' he replied, 'I remind myself that every person is a child of God, and is therefore of great value. And I just try always to put the best possible connotation on everything he does or says. As a result, I get to liking him, and I guess he takes a liking to me, too.' Of course, you'll not be surprised to know that this man has a good day every day.

Practice Self-improvement

What I have tried to do is open you up to a 'spiritual awakening.' It may happen quickly and dramatically. On the other hand, it may be a developing experience unfolding as the rose, beginning with the bud and ending with the full flowering. In either case, you will have that feeling described in the words: 'Were not our hearts strangely warmed within us.'

This is the greatest experience possible to a human being. Tolstoy described it in an immortal phrase. 'To know God is to live.' The result is a transformed, changed life — the ultimate in personality improvement. Now what final steps can you take to have this, the most important of all human experiences? Here they are.

Realise that you have already begun the process of spiritual experience if you have followed the lessons in this book. You are already practicing self-improvement and spiritual change.

Give up everything that is wrong. Now give up everything in your life that you know in your heart is wrong. You cannot rationalise if you want full spiritual power. I must remind you that, in your self-improvement plan, you have now arrived at the moment when change must be made.

Forgive and forget. Eliminate from your heart forever all hatred, resentment, jealousy and grudges. You must sincerely forgive everyone against whom you hold resentment.

Make amends. Make amends for any wrong you have done to other persons. If no amends are possible, pray that God in His own way will make it right for you. Then ask to be forgiven. Believe that the matter is cancelled out and forget it.

Realise that you are changed. Realise that you are changed not by any act you perform, but through faith in God, who alone can make you a new person. You can improve yourself by diligent practice, but the final act of personality improvement is a gift conferred upon you through humble faith in God.

Start to live a new life. Start to live a new life. This may not be easy at first. But if you simply start living the new life assuming that you will be successful and keep living it, you will be successful. Start living the glorious new life today and believe that with God's help you are going forward to better things. Believe that every day will see you stronger and happier. For a life of inner peace and power, start now and you have such a life — now.

Believe that God has heard your prayer and granted your request. Accept the fact that you are now a 'new creature,' a transformed person.

What is the Power to Change Your Life?

This amazing power is the life of God in you. It is a force that, when focussed, produces spectacular changes in the personality. The person who feels weak, ineffective, defeated and sinful has within himself a stored-up force that can effect enormous change. But he cannot do it on his own. He must have the releasing action that comes through the simple act of giving his life to God.

When this self-giving is done with real sincerity, spiritual power will take over your life. The spirit of God will flow into you and fill your life with joy and contentment.

Chapter 5

Enthusiasm
what it can do for you

Nothing great was ever achieved
without enthusiasm.

— *Ralph Waldo Emerson*

*E*nthusiasm is no simple, sweet, or easy concept. It is a strong, rugged mental attitude that is hard to come by, difficult to maintain, but powerful.

The word enthusiasm from the Greek *entheos* means God in you, or full of God. So when we claim for enthusiasm the power to work miracles in solving problems, we are actually saying that God Himself in you supplies the wisdom, courage, and faith necessary to deal successfully with all difficulties. We need only to discover how to apply efficiency and right thinking enthusiastically to our problems.

Because enthusiasm is so vitally important as a life motivation, and makes a vast difference in one's life, Emerson wrote: 'Nothing great was ever achieved without enthusiasm.'

Enthusiasm overcomes apathy, according to the famous historian Arnold Toynbee, who said, 'Apathy can only be overcome by enthusiasm, and enthusiasm can only be aroused by two things; first, an ideal which takes the imagination by storm, and second, a definite intelligible plan for carrying that ideal into practice.'

There is an extraordinary, dynamic quality about enthusiasm. It is permeated by a victorious attitude so powerful that it sweeps all before it. It brings the personality alive, releasing dormant powers.

Walt Whitman, great American poet, tells us that he found himself and set himself free through enthusiasm. He said, 'I was simmering, really simmering; Emerson brought me to a boil.' So many of us continue to simmer in our ineffectiveness, until some profound motivation awakens us to the true possibilities inherent within us.

The difference between enthusiasm and faith is very slight indeed. Perhaps enthusiasm may be defined as faith that has been set afire. A pathetic fact is that not a few people go through their days without zest. There is little or no thrill to their lives. As a result, they are sadly lacking in the power to meet and overcome difficulties victoriously. They age and grow old before their time. Continuing vitality is dependent upon aliveness of spirit. Thoreau's warning should not go unheeded: 'None are so old as those who have out-lived enthusiasm.'

Practice Enthusiasm and Have It

Enthusiasm is one of God's greatest gifts.

What is the outstanding characteristic of a little child? It is enthusiasm! He thinks the world is terrific; he just loves it, everything fascinates him. Huxley said that the secret of genius is to carry the spirit of the child into old age, which means never losing your enthusiasm. But all too few persons retain this excitement and a reason is they let enthusiasm be drained off. If you are not getting as much from life as you want to, then examine the state of your enthusiasm.

My mother was one of the most enthusiastic persons I ever knew. She got an enormous thrill out of the most ordinary events. She had the ability to see romance and glory in everything. She travelled the world over. I recall one foggy night, when she and I were crossing from New Jersey to New York City on a ferry boat. To me, there was nothing particularly beautiful about fog seen from a ferry boat, but my mother exclaimed, 'Isn't this thrilling?'

'What is thrilling?' I asked.

'Why,' she said, 'the fog, the lights, the other ferry boat we just passed! Look at the mysterious way its lights fade into the mist.'

Just then, we heard the sound of a foghorn, deep-throated in the heavy, padded whiteness of the mist. My mother's face was that of an excited child. I had felt nothing about this ride except that I was in a hurry to get across the river. She stood at the rail that night and eyed me appraisingly. 'Norman,' she said gently, 'I have been giving you advice all your life. Some of it you have taken; some you haven't. But here is some I want you to take. Make up your mind, right now, that the world is a-thrill with beauty and excitement. Keep yourself sensitized to it. Love the world, its beauty, and its people.' Anybody trying consistently to follow that simple course will be blessed with abundant enthusiasm and have a life full of joy.

Try the 'As If' Principle

You can deliberately make yourself enthusiastic. To make yourself into whatever type of person you wish to be, first, decide specifically what particular characteristic you desire to possess and then hold that image firmly in consciousness. Second, proceed to develop it by acting as if you actually possessed the desired characteristic. And, third, believe and repeatedly affirm that you are in the process of self-creating the quality you wish to develop. In this way, you use the 'As if' principle.

William James, who taught this principle, said: 'If you want a quality, act as if you already had it.' Shakespeare tells us in Act III of *Hamlet*, 'Assume a virtue, if you have it not.'

Frank Bettger, a top insurance man, was once dropped from a job for one reason only — lack of enthusiasm. 'You must have enthusiasm. It's primary requisite for success,' he was told.

'But,' complained Bettger, 'what can I do? I haven't got enthusiasm. You just can't go out and buy it in a store. You either have it, or you don't. I haven't, so that's it, I guess.'

'You're wrong; make yourself act enthusiastic. It's as simple as that. Act with enthusiasm and soon you will have enthusiasm. Once you're fired with conviction, your natural talents will take you to the top.'

'Miss Nobody'

One night, I met 'Miss Nobody.' After a speech in a West Coast city, a young woman gave me a limp handshake and said in a small, timid voice, 'I thought I'd like to shake hands with you, but I really shouldn't be bothering you. There are so many important people here and I'm just a nobody.'

'Please remain. I'd like to talk with you.' Later I said, 'now, Miss Nobody let's have a little visit.'

'What did you call me?' she asked in surprise.

'I called you by the only name you gave. You told me you were a Nobody. Have you another name?'

'Of course,' she said. 'You see, I have quite an inferiority complex. I came to hear you, hoping you might say something that would help me.'

'Well,' I answered, 'I'm saying it to you now: You are a child of God.' And I advised her to draw herself up tall each day and say to herself, 'I am a child of God.' I outlined for her some of the techniques in this book for practicing enthusiasm and self-confidence.

Recently, speaking in the same area, an attractive young woman approached, 'Do you remember me? I'm the former Miss Nobody.' Her enthusiastic manner and the sparkle in her eyes showed her change.

This incident underscores an important fact. You can change! Anybody can change! And even from a dull nobody to an enthusiastic somebody.

Tell Yourself Good News

To develop enthusiasm, start the day right. You can condition a day in the first five minutes after you wake up. Henry Thoreau used to lie abed in the morning, telling himself all the good news he could think of. Then he arose to meet the day in a world filled with good things, good people, good opportunities.

The late William H. Danforth, a prominent business leader, said, 'Every morning pull yourself up to your full height and stand tall. Then think tall — think great, elevated thoughts. Then go out and act tall. Do that and joy will flow to you.'

Go on spreading enthusiasm all day, and at night you will have a deposit of joy in your life such as you never had before.

Love Life and People To Be Enthusiastic

One magic formula for successful and enthusiastic living is stated in six powerful words: *find a need and fill it*. Every enterprise that has achieved success has been predicated on that formula.

Find people's needs, fill them. Love people. Love the sky, love beauty, love God. The person who loves always becomes enthusiastic. If you're not enthusiastic, begin today to cultivate the love of living. Like Fred, for example, who runs a little eating place.

Resting a big hand on the counter, he asked me, 'Okay, brother, what'll you have?'

'Are you Fred?'

'Yep.'

'They tell me you have good hamburgers.'

'Brother, you never ate such hamburgers.'

'Okay, let me have one.'

Along the counter was an old man who looked extremely miserable. He was sitting hunched over. His hand shook. After Fred had put my hamburger in front of me, he went over and put his hand on that of this old fellow. 'That's all right, Bill,' he said. 'That's all right. I'm going to fix you a bowl of that nice hot soup that you like.' Bill nodded gratefully.

Another old man got up and shuffled over to pay his check. Fred said, 'Mr. Brown, watch out for the cars out there on the avenue. They come pretty fast at night.' And he added, 'Have a look at the moonlight on the river. It's mighty pretty tonight.'

When I paid my check, I couldn't help remarking, 'You know something, my friend? I like the way you spoke to those old men. You made them feel that life is good.'

'Why not?' he asked. 'Life *is* good. Me, I get a kick out of living. They're pretty sad old guys and our place is sort of like home to them. Anyway, I kind of like' em.'

Believe in yourself. Practice the principles of enthusiasm. Find needs and fill them. Believe that you can be better than you think you are. And remember — if you think you can, you can! Bring bona fide enthusiasm to your life-style — for enthusiasm always makes the difference.

Learn to 'Fail Forward'

The enthusiast has enormous resources that will equate with all problems. This does not mean that the enthusiast will not have his hard moments. He may even fail at times. Everybody does. But he learns some thing from failure. He 'fails forward,' and uses his failure creatively in the direction of eventual success.

You have heard the expression, 'If life hands you a lemon, make lemonade.' This is another way of saying, 'fail forward.' Enthusiasm keeps you from letting problems overwhelm you.

I know a man who manages hotel. He so inspires his staff that all are vitally alive and enthusiastic. One day I was strolling with him along a path called 'Philosopher's Walk.'

'I like to take this walk,' he said. 'As a boy, I worked in the kitchens of a large hotel in Chicago, so I didn't get much schooling. But I learned to read such great thinkers as Marcus Aurelius, William James, Emerson, Socrates, Plato and, above all, Jesus. The hotel business can be very exasperating. But I found that, if I fill my mind with such thoughts as those great men teach, I can do my job and love it.'

A few days later, when a guest's bath overflowed and water came through the beautiful ceiling of the lobby, I found the manager pacing up and down Philosopher's Walk. 'I am getting myself conditioned to talk to the lady who overflowed her bathtub,' he explained.

When that woman left, she asked to return the next year, saying she had never received such understanding treatment. That man was able to maintain enthusiasm for his job with its exasperations through cultivated thought control. That happens when you develop a sense of enthusiasm for your job.

Give Yourself To Find Yourself

I spoke to two thousand men at a convention of insurance agents. Seated beside the president of the association, I noted what a dynamic individual he was. He exuded energy, enthusiasm, and vitality. I was greatly impressed, and asked him just how he came by all that aliveness.

'Five years ago, I was a sleepy, unsuccessful life insurance agent. I was failing at everything. I was a member of our church back home, but I wasn't a good member.

'Then the pastor asked me to be chairman of the church finance committee. He sure was scraping the bottom of the barrel, because what did I know about church finances? I was failing in my own job and in financial difficulty personally. But, for some reason, the minister picked me. He told me the Lord had this job for me to do. That was the only time I had any doubts about Divine Wisdom. I said, "Where am I going to get the information on what to do?" The pastor said, "Read the Bible and do what it says."

'To my surprise, I found that the Bible is a great book on economics. It made me a tither — giving ten percent of my time and money to the Lord. I recovered enthusiasm. My shattered personality came together. Everything changed for the better. That's why I'm so upbeat in spirit.'

The more you give of yourself, the more you will find yourself. Give yourself to people. Pray for everybody. Give more time to the service of God and your fellow man. Give of your money, of your life. Life will come flooding back to you, life and excitement such as you never felt before. Try it. It will work.

Let Go and Let God

The writer H. W. Arnold tells us: 'The worst bankrupt is the man who has lost his enthusiasm. Let a man lose everything in the world but his enthusiasm, and he will come through again to success.' To keep full of enthusiasm, as God intended you to be, keep your intake of energy greater than the outgo of energy. If you are tense, uptight, the constant tension depletes you so that energy dissipates and with it your enthusiasm. Therefore, discover the great technique of being able to 'let go and let God.' Ask God for wisdom and guidance, and then give to your job the very best. Having done your best, leave the outcome to the Lord, trusting in His providence. You will find renewal, new energy, new enthusiasm.

Enthusiasm Changes Job Situations

Enthusiasm makes the difference in work performance. Expose your daily occupation to apathy, and your job will be difficult and tiresome. No job will go well for the person who considers it just another dull chore.

The secret of genius is to carry the spirit of child into old age.

— *Huxley*

You may say, 'My job is dull and has no future.' But might it be that you have a dull attitude toward it? Try enthusiasm and watch it change. And see how you change with it. Enthusiasm changes a job because it changes the job holder. When you apply enthusiasm to the job, the job comes alive with exciting new possibilities. So if you wish for a new job, try instead to apply enthusiasm to your present one that will make it new.

For instance, ask what someone else might see in your job. Consider what he or she would do with it. Perhaps that person is doing exceedingly well in his own work. Try to imagine what he would do if suddenly he took over your job. How do you think he would react toward it? What fresh and innovative changes would he make to put new life and achievement into what you consider a dull job? Then apply those ideas.

Change Your Job ... With Enthusiasm

Enthusiasm is important to success. The president of a big company said, 'If I am trying to decide between two men of fairly equal ability and one man definitely has enthusiasm, I know he will go farther, for enthusiasm has self-releasing power and carries all before it.'

Certainly! A man with enthusiasm always wants to learn. He gives the job all he's got, throws everything into it. A man with enthusiasm is constantly releasing himself.

Attitudes Are More Important Than Facts

Enthusiasm helps work miracles in problems because enthusiasm is an attitude of mind, and the mental attitude in a difficult situation is the important factor in its solution. Attitudes are more important than facts. Enthusiasm changes the mental outlook of fearing facts to the solid assurance that there is an answer. One man looking at a tough problem says glumly, 'There are the facts. There is nothing I can do but accept them.' So the facts have him defeated. Another man, blessed with an enthusiastic attitude, seeing the same facts, says, 'Sure those are the facts all right, and they are indeed tough. But I never yet saw a set of difficult facts to which there was not a solution. Perhaps some facts cannot be changed, but maybe I can bypass or weave them into a new pattern, or readjust my strategy. If necessary, I can lie with them and ultimately use them to advantage.' That man's attitude brings the magic of creative believing into play. These words can make an amazing difference in your life: *Every problem contains within itself the seeds of its own solution.* The enthusiast described above knows this great truth.

Enthusiasm Equal to the Toughest Problems

In a city, two men took me to a prayer group meeting late one night. On the way, one of them said, 'A year ago, we were a couple of drunks. But now we've got hold of something that has really changed us.'

Some 50 people were gathered for the prayer meeting. They were sitting everywhere; three were even perched on the grand piano. A man was playing the piano and I'm sure he would have been a success in any nightclub. They were going from one hymn to another, singing until the sound threatened to raise the roof. Then all started to pray. A thrill like an electric charge went around among all the people during that prayer period.

A man and a woman stood up and testified: 'We were breaking up our marriage. We were unfaithful to each other and we fought like cats and dogs. Now, we love each other, and we are sorry for what we were. But we have been lifted to a higher level.'

'Who did this for you?' I asked.

'Jesus,' they said, quietly.

Then a very beautiful woman stood and said, 'I was an addict. I got so bad that one time I was picked up from the street where I lay in the gutter.'

I exclaimed, 'A beautiful girl like you?'

'Do you think so? It was Jesus who did it for me.'

It was well after 3 a.m. when I got back to my room at the hotel and I had to catch an airplane at five o'clock. I did not go to bed at all that night. I did not need sleep. I was full of joy and energy and enthusiasm!

A man I met at a convention remarked. 'How can I learn the magic of believing — the power of enthusiasm?'

'Figure out a method of your own for practicing the magic of believing?'

I suggested. 'You will find that it works and enthusiasm will be yours.'

Here was his solution: Like many executives, he had on his desk a receptacle for incoming mail and other paper, and a second container for outgoing mail and papers. To this he added a third receptacle labeled, 'With God All Things Are Possible.' In this one, he placed all matters for which he did not yet have answers and problems for which no solution had been determined. To use his own phrase, he held these matters in 'prayerful thinking. I surround the problems in that box with the magic of believing and the results are amazing.'

Use Self-Motivators

W. Clement Stone was a genuinely enthusiastic person. I once asked him the secret of his enthusiasm.

'As you know,' he answered, 'the emotions are not always immediately subject to reason, but they are always immediately subject to action (mental or physical). Furthermore, repetition of the same thought or physical action develops into a habit that repeated frequently enough, becomes an automatic reflex.

'And that's why I use self-motivators. A self-motivator is an affirmation that you deliberately use to move yourself to desirable action. You repeat a verbal self-motivator fifty times in the morning... fifty times at night... for a week or ten days, to imprint the words indelibly in your memory.

'If a personal problem involves deep emotions, I always use man's greatest power immediately... the power of prayer. In solving business problems, I will also pray for guidance, but not necessarily immediately.'

For Mr. Stone, enthusiasm makes the difference.

The Contagion of Enthusiasm

'Enthusiasm, like measles, mumps, and the common cold, is highly contagious,' says the writer Emory Ward.

But, unlike measles and mumps and colds, enthusiasm is good for you. Hope you catch it, and good.

When contagious, enthusiastic faith in yourself releases you change and, as you change, your whole life from the self-built prison of your mind; then you begin to change and, as you change, your whole life changes also. Buddha said, 'The mind is everything. What you think you become.' Perhaps you are being overwhelmed by your problems. They have you disorganized and confused. There is Someone concerned about you. God will help you to turn about, march forward, and win the battle. Heed His challenge, follow His leadership, and you will be filled with enthusiasm. And as you meet your problems, they will give way before your enthusiasm and positive faith.

Enthusiasm Has Lifting Power

Let me tell you about one experience with the contagion of enthusiasm. As an introduction to my speech at a convention in Chicago, a skit was used.

The leading character was a businessman. In this little play, he answered certain questions put to him by the others and, at the same time, gave a moving witness of what God had done for him. He told of the troubles he had faced in business; how life had become hard for him and he became nervous, tense, and ineffective; how his doctor had finally told him he faced a nervous breakdown unless he could somehow find himself. Then he related how he had found God. In a simple, unaffected manner, and in everyday, down-to-earth language, he told how this wonderful thing had come into his life.

The room was filled with about four thousand people and it was late in the morning, after a number of speeches. Yet you could almost hear the stillness, you could feel the rapt attention.

I became aware of something coming up out of the audience, a lifting power, an indescribable, indefinable force, something intangible but very real, that had power in it. It held the quality of joy. It was deep, dynamic

Self-motivators

- *Serious personal problem:* God is always a good God!
- *Business problem:* You have a problem... that's good!
- Within every adversity there is a seed of an equivalent or greater benefit.
- What the mind can conceive and believe, the mind can achieve.
- Find one good idea that will work and... work that one idea!
- Do it now!
- To be enthusiastic... ACT... enthusiastically!

enthusiasm — an audience lifted and conditioned by a man's simple story of a tremendous spiritual experience.

Later in the day, I met a physician who had been present at this meeting. He remarked, 'A strange thing happened. As I listened to that man, I said to myself, "This is a therapeutic thing. All unhealthy thoughts are being driven out of the minds of all these people. There is healing power in this place."'

Let Enthusiasm Take Hold!

I knew Vince Lombardi, the fabulous football coach. When he came to Green Bay, he faced a defeated, dispirited team. He stood before them, looked them over silently for a long time, and then in a quiet but intense way said, 'Gentlemen, we are going to have a great football team. We are going to win games. Get that. You are going to learn to block. You are going to learn to run. You are going to learn to tackle. You are going to out play the teams that come against you. Get that.

'And how is this to be done?' he continued. 'You are to have confidence in me and enthusiasm for my system. The secret of the whole matter will be what goes on up here. (And he tapped his temple.) Here-after, I want you to think of only three things: Your home, your religion, and the Green Bay Packers, in that order! Let enthusiasm take hold of you!'

The men sat up straight in their chairs. 'I walked out of that meeting,' wrote the quarterback, 'feeling ten feet tall!' That year, they won seven games — with virtually the same players who had lost ten games the year before. The next year, they won a Division title, and the third year the World Championship. Why? Because, added to hard work and skill and love of the sport, enthusiasm made the difference.

What happened to the Green Bay Packers can happen to a church, to a business, to a country, to an individual. What goes on in the mind is what determines outcome. When an individual really gets enthusiasm, you can see it in the flash of his eyes, in his alert and vibrant personality. You observe it in the spring of his step. You can see it in the verve of his whole being. Enthusiasm makes the difference in his attitude toward his job, toward other people, toward the world. It make a great big difference in the zest and delight of human existence.

Action Steps

1. Like mumps, it can be caught, so expose yourself to enthusiasm people.
2. Start thinking enthusiasm and positive thoughts about yourself.
3. Let others catch enthusiasm from you.

Enthusiasm can Remake Your Life

The kind of living that makes life good is as exact as a science, and not something that you just muddle through without following rules. Life responds to certain precise methods and procedures. Your life can be either a miss or a hit, can either be empty or full, depending on how you go at it. And the enthusiastic knows and draws upon the resources. He plays it cool and straight. Finally, he believes there is nothing in life so difficult that it can't be overcome. This faith can move mountains. It can change people. It can change the world. You can survive all the great storms in your life.

However, enthusiasm is a quality that must be affirmed and reaffirmed. Donald Curtis suggests that you affirm each morning: 'I move serenely forward into the adventure of life today. I am filled with inspiration and enthusiasm. I am guided and protected by the Infinite in everything I say and do. I project confidence and authority. I am sure of myself in every situation. With God's help, I am filled with the strength and energy to be what I am and to do what I have to do...'

Keep Enthusiasm and Nothing Can Break You

I once visited a brass foundry. A man showed me how they heated the molten brass to a temperature of 2200 degrees Fahrenheit. It was heated in huge graflex crucibles. The intense heat made the whole crucible glow incandescently. Then, pointing to a crucible out of which this molten metal had only just been poured and which therefore was still red hot, the man said 'Let me show you something.' He took an enormous sledge and, using all his force, smote this red-hot empty crucible again and again. The only effect was a few almost imperceptible dents, so resilient was the graflex at high temperature.

Then he showed me a crucible that had been allowed to cool and he took a small hammer and, with a flex of his wrist, hit this cold crucible a few times-and it shattered into a hundred pieces! 'When it's cold,' he said 'it's brittle.'

'People are like those crucibles. When they are surcharged with spiritual fire and enthusiasm, nothing can break them. But if they let the spiritual fire and enthusiasm die down, then even small blows of circumstance can crack and shatter them.'

He Learned to Practice Enthusiasm

Suppose life has dealt harshly, and the zest, eagerness, thrill, and enthusiasm have gone out of you. How do you recover them? By one of the greatest devices God ever made — by rebirth. Once I had dinner with a group of 20 men, ten ministers and ten laymen. One man in particular was a master storyteller. I remarked to the minister sitting next to me, 'This character really has something.'

'He surely has,' the minister replied. 'He's a member of my church. And he's my Exhibit A.'

'What do you mean, "Exhibit A"?'

'You should have seen him a few years ago. He was go gripey and crabbed, people avoided him. He had pains around the heart, he had pains up the arm, he was short of breath. He was a hypochondriac. And he haunted doctors' offices one after another. He took more pills than anybody in town. But they didn't seem to help him. He had built up a splendid business. Yet he was never happy.

'Finally, a doctor shipped him off to a specialist in Chicago. And this Chicago specialist was a wise man. He told our friend, "These pains of yours are pseudo pains. They do not come from any physical origin: they are induced by wrong, unhealthy thinking. Get your thinking changed, start living a vital enthusiastic life — and you'll be well. That is my prescription. Fifteen hundred dollars, please."

'Our friend exclaimed, "Fifteen hundred buck! For what?"

' "For knowing what to tell you. You charge plenty in your business. So do I.' (The doctor later explained he knew this man wouldn't value advice unless he had to pay for it.)

So this maladjusted man returned home and went immediately to his minister, saying, 'That doctor in Chicago told me to get my thinking straightened out. You know, that fellow is a highwayman! He charged me fifteen hundred dollars! So how do I get my thinking straightened out? I'll get my fifteen hundred dollars' worth if it kills me!' (Which is precisely what the doctor had foreseen.)

The minister said, 'Okay, Jim, how far do you live from here? Five miles? I see your chauffeur sitting out there in your car. Call him and dismiss him. I want you to walk home. And as you walk, thank God for those feet of yours, thank God for your legs, thank God that you went to Chicago and were told you have a sound body. Walk home practicing enthusiasm for life, for yourself, for the pine forest you pass on the way, for all your friends, for your church, for God. And tomorrow I want you to walk back and tell me how you feel.'

Eventually, the man got wise and asked the minister to walk with him. The minister walked with him all in all a good 25 miles until, one day, he challenged the man, 'Why don't you let go and let the God take over?' And he did.

'That is your storyteller,' the minister told me in conclusion. 'Exhibit A. He learned to practice enthusiasm and he is a well man — a happy man.'

Every morning, you have a new set of facts. Some of them are new forms of old facts. And that is what you have to work with.

Walk in Newness of Life

Maybe our forefathers grew great and strong because they drew strength from the sky and the hills and the streams — the forces and the wonders of nature. Enthusiastic men are men who live in relationship with nature and with nature's God. So activate your mind and let it flow out and become an alive part of the world, thrill to the world, thrill to people. Heed the Bible, which tells us we should 'walk in newness of life.' That is a powerful idea. We're not supposed to be old, dead, dull, desultory. Enthusiasm can remake your life!

Action Steps

1. Stop running yourself down. There's a lot that's right in you. Empty your mind of your failures and mistakes and start respecting yourself.

2. Eliminate self-pity. Start thinking of what you have left, instead of dwelling on what you have lost. List your assets on a piece of paper.
3. Quit thinking of yourself. Think of helping others. Actually go out and find someone who needs the kind of help you can give and give it. For you will never have a continuing flow of abundance if your thought is only for yourself.
4. Remember Goethe: 'He who has a firm will mold the world to himself.' Almighty God put a tough thing into human beings called the will. Use it.
5. Have a goal and put a timetable on it.
6. Stop wasting your mental energy on gripes and postmortems, and start thinking about what to do now. Amazing things happen, when you think constructively.
7. Every morning and every evening of your life, articulate these words: 'I can do all things through God who strengthens me'
8. Every day three times say: 'This is the day the Lord has made. I will rejoice and be glad in it'.

# Chapter 6

Courage
finding your strength in troubled times

Courage is fear that has said
its prayer.

*Y*ou don't need to go through life in a spirit of fear. I tell you in the name of God you don't. How can you be free of it? I will answer in four words: FAITH CANCELS OUT FEAR. Faith is stronger than fear, much stronger. When fear comes, counter it with an affirmation of faith: Fear no evil, for God is with you.

Love overcomes fear. Acting lovingly will promote trust, confidence and dependence on God. Live with the thought of being in God's care — of Him loving you — and you will develop a sound mind where no shadowy fear can lurk. You will open wide the gate to confident living.

Suppose the Lord were with you right now, sitting in the same room with you, or walking alongside you as you go from place to place so that you feel His shoulder alongside yours, hear the sound of His footsteps and look into His face. Then would you be afraid? Of course not. Well, He is there when you have Him in your heart and when you truly believe that He wants the best for you.

Consider what putting on 'God's full armour' really means to you. By arming yourself in faith in the way an ancient warrior prepared himself for battle, you can face life's toughest challenges — the 'evil day.'

Today's armour is put on by girding yourself with truth. When encircled with truth, nothing can get through your spiritual defenses to defeat you. The breastplate of righteousness is the assurance you get from goodness and rightmindedness. Take up the shield of faith to protect your heart, your vital center. When you have faith in your heart, your life center is protected. The helmet of salvation will clear your head of negative thoughts. Finally, seize the sword of the spirit, the bright and shining sword of God's power and with it strike out against evil.

Put on God's full armour, be strong in the Lord and feel the power of His might.

Hope

You're never defeated, never beaten down as long as you have hope. Keep this thought in mind always as difficulties, sorrow, sickness and trouble come upon you. Have you heard that old saying that where there is life, there is hope? I suggest you turn it around: where there is hope, there is life. Form a picture in your mind, not of lack or denial or frustration or illness, but of prosperity, abundance, attainment, health. You will receive as a result of prayer exactly what you think, not what you say. Therefore, practice believing even as you pray that you will receive god's boundless blessings — that they are already on their way to you. When you live with hope

We are not creatures of circumstances; we are creators of circumstances.

— *Benjamin Disraeli*

in your heart, in your mind and in your spirit, you have discovered one of life's most powerful secrets.

Assurance

When you are filled with despair and doubt your ability to rid yourself of it, don't say to yourself, 'I can't do it; I haven't got it in me.' On the contrary, you have a very big 'it' within you. You have only to believe in the strength God has placed in each of us to release it and make it work in your life.

One of the most powerful traits in human nature is that when you maintain a mental attitude of trust and faith — when you hope, dream, believe, pray and work toward God's assurance — you will create conditions in which every good thing can come to you. Fill your mind with the positive power of spiritual expectancy, and God and His good will come into your life.

Comfort

No matter how dark it gets, how lonely or dejected you feel, you are not alone. Whenever anxiety or disappointments come, repeat: 'I am not alone. God is with me.' Thank God constantly for watching over you. After every journey thank Him for His protecting care. In every difficult situation thank Him for seeing you through.

Visualise yourself and your loved ones as always being protected by the everlasting arms of God and supported by His great hand. Remember: God alone is steadfast and unchanging in a world of pain and insecurity. Because God loves you and is always with you, you can have confidence that, if you live His way to the best of your ability and put your trust in Him, you will endure.

Trust

We live on a trust basis every day. We trust the motorman of a train, the driver of bus, the cook in a restaurant. We put our lives completely into the hands of these people, and usually, we don't even know them. Here we are on this earth, a whirling island in the sky, wholly dependent on God without giving our total dependence on Him much thought. Yet He is the only One deserving our complete trust.

When you ask God for an answer to a prayer, never doubt that you will get a perfect answer. One reason we do not get answers to our prayers is that we ask, but do not really *expect* to receive. We are expert askers, but inexpert receivers.

How may we trust God in life's daily affairs? One way is to know and love God.

When you know God, His goodness, kindness and faithfulness, you will trust Him. When you feel uncertain, say the following to yourself:

> I put my life in God's hands.
>   I will trust God's guidance.
> I leave the outcome to God.

Believe that God has all the answers to your troubles. Don't be afraid to do what He guides you to do. Trust Him.

Patience

If you had to make a choice between God's time and your time, which would you choose? I thought so. So, rest in the Lord. Don't think you can handle everything on your own. Don't let the tension and tumult of present-day living distract you from waiting on God's perfect timing.

God will see to it that all you really need, you can have. But it has been said that the mills of the God's grind slowly. Picture a great wheel dipping into the stream of history, a great wheel that keeps rolling with a slow and certain motion. Think of this slow and certain wheel as God's wheel. It never makes mistakes; it is unerring. Its slow, sure movement will grind out justice. God doesn't always win in a hurry, but He always wins.

Perseverance

Never talk defeat, for if you do you can talk yourself into accepting it. Do not hug the shore; do not fear high places. Think high and wide and deep and far. Mohammed said, 'God is with those who persevere,' and Shakespeare observed that 'much rain wears the marble.'

When I was a boy, after an especially gloomy session in Algebra class, I informed my mother that I would never understand it. 'I just can't get it. I can't, I can't.' She fixed me with level gaze and said, sharply and crisply, words that have served me ever since: 'You can if you think you can.' What power lies within these words and in *you* when you truly believe them.

Do you have a big goal, an impossible dream? Then let your faith rise up as an eagle in the sky; believe in your dream, believe God wants you to have it. Think high and wide and deep and far, and God will lead you to your dream.

Chapter 7

How to make a new start

Adversity causes some men to break, others to break records.

— *William A. Ward*

One of the best things any of us can do is to deliberately, intensely, and sincerely make a new start in life. Whether you have a serious, deep problem to overcome or simply wish to breathe new life into your everyday routine, this chapter is designed to help.

Many people do not believe they can begin again. They insist that their situation is so bad that they can do nothing about it. But I am such a firm believer in the power of God, in the opportunities all around us, and in the greatness that is in people, that I believe anyone can do amazing things. And that includes you!

The aim of this chapter is to give the inspiration and the tools you will need to make a new start, to help put the past behind you, and to infuse your mind and thoughts with new energy and resolve. Whoever you are, whatever your circumstance, you *can* begin again!

You may be thinking that, because you are too old, or your situation is too hopeless, or you don't have the resources you need, you cannot start over again. If that is what you believe, you simply do not realize the ideas and the comeback power you have inside you. You do not know the tremendous things you can do.

Believe in your power to change, and you have taken the first step toward a new start.

Once you have taken that important first step, you must discover how to keep that new start going. In the beginning, you will probably feel a sense of enthusiasm and determination. But, as the days pass, your motivation may subside. Unless you are careful, you will be back in the same old desultory groove. To keep a new start going, constantly feed positive ideas into your attitude. You and I can do anything we want with life — if we keep our attitudes strong and vital.

A teenager who was plagued by an attitude of self-doubt once spoke with Fiorello La Guardia, then mayor of New York City, about her lack of self-confidence. His cryptic reply restored faith in herself and remained with her always: 'Listen to me, young lady. I know what I'm talking about. Trust God, believe in yourself, and you can do anything.' That is a fact. Through faith, in God and in yourself, you can do almost anything.

As you read you will experience renewed energy and confidence. By following these suggestions and drawing upon God's help, you will discover the real power of positive thinking. As you do so, you will change, and grow and become all you dream of becoming.

Re-Discover Your Genius

A science magazine once published an article that, though startling, seemed to me quite significant. The more I dwell on it, the more it seems true, at least within limits. The article declared that all normal children possess, in their infancy, qualities of genius. Mediocrity, it claims, does not appear until later in life. Children, says the article, are geniuses in miniature.

If that is so, what happens to the genius in most of us? Some people develop genius; others sadly lose it. Or do they? No, you never lose anything; nothing is ever destroyed; nothing is ever forgotten. Everything you have ever seen, thought, or experienced is filed away in your mind. The genius you were born with is still there, covered up, buried. Given the proper combination of circumstances and the great insight of spiritual power it can be released.

What you become depends on you. God has given you the ability to overcome all difficulties, to meet all situations. But you must learn to think creatively and positively, before you can begin to get any where in life. To make a new start, re-examine your mental attitudes, your motivation, and your spiritual thought habits. In short, how strong is your faith?

Know What you Want

To get what you want in life, you must first *know* what you want.

I stopped one day at a petrol station. The young man who cleaned my windshield recognized me and asked if he could talk with me. I pulled my car away from the petrol station and asked, 'What is on your mind?'

'Look at my job,' he said. 'Wiping windshields, putting air in tires, filling tanks. I'm sick of it.'

'It is not very fascinating,' I agreed, 'but there is nothing more satisfying than a clean windshield.' I was trying to sell him on how wonderful it is to clean a windshield right. But that created no enthusiasm.

'I want to get somewhere,' he said plaintively.

'That is the way I like to hear a man talk,' I said. 'Precisely where do you want to get?'

'I don't know exactly,' he admitted. 'But I want to get somewhere.'

'What can you do best?' I asked.

'I've never thought about that,' he replied. 'I guess I don't do anything very well.'

When asked what he would *like* to do, he answered that he didn't know.

'Jack,' I said, 'you are going nowhere until you know where you want to go, what you can do best, what you would like to do. At that point, dedicate yourself and your desires to God, and you will begin to get somewhere.'

Compare Jack's story to that of a newspaper editor I knew. 'How did you get to be editor of this paper?' I asked him, for I knew he had known poverty.

'I wanted to be,' was his answer.

Believe in your power to change,
and you have taken the first step
toward a new start.

'You wanted to be an editor and so you became one?'

'That's all there is to it,' he explained. 'I used to visit the newspaper office and look at the editor and feel sorry for him, because I knew I was going to take his place. And,' he added, 'I printed that thought on my consciousness. I wrote on a sheet of paper, "I am the future editor of this newspaper," and propped it up in front of me in my room. I had it in my notebooks in school.'

What do you think happened? Why, one day as a young man, he got a job as a printer's devil, or apprentice, the lowliest of the low. And he gave it all he had. He learned the newspaper business from the bottom to the top. That is how Roger Ferger became editor of the Cincinnati *Enquirer*.

Find yourself.

There are people everywhere who have never found themselves. We have selves that hide behind all kinds of inferiority and resentment feelings, selves that never get out from our own self-doubt, selves that are like birds in a cage. We fail to become what God meant us to be. And it is a terrible thing to go through life and never really find yourself.

I had a conversation with a woman who has achieved a distinguished and noteworthy career. I asked her about her family background.

'I never knew who my parents were,' she said. 'And I had only three years of schooling.'

Yet she became one of New York City's most successful businesswomen.

'The first job I had was working in a cotton mill in the south, sweeping up,' she told me. 'I came up from that.' 'What became of the other women who worked with you?' I asked. 'Did you never hear anything about them?'

'No,' she said. 'I never did.'

Why did this woman come up and not the others? That is one of the most interesting questions about human nature. My theory is that those other women never found themselves, never questioned what they wanted out of life, never believed in themselves. They were never set free within themselves. They yielded to a difficult environment and were crushed by it.

Understand Success

Sometime ago, I was making an overnight journey with a friend whose mind is occupied almost continuously with one question. He seeks information on that subject from nearly everyone he meets.

'Why is it,' he asks, 'that some people succeed while others fail?' Then he relates instances of unlikely people succeeding and the same kinds of people failing.

His definition of success is mine also, as I am sure it is yours. Success is not a matter of money. Haven't we all known people who, possessing a great deal of money, are failures as people? And haven't we all seen people with little money who are also failures?

Then there is the notion that every person who has achieved fame is a success. I used to believe that myself. If I saw a man's name in the newspaper, I thought he was a success. If I saw his picture, too, I was sure he was a *big* success. But my mother used to say that most of the people you read about in the papers are not successful. They have just done something different, or something bad. And, in time, I came to agree with her. If you lead a decent, respectable life, that is not news. But if you don't, that is one way to get your name in the papers.

The way to live successfully is not complicated, nor is it all that difficult. Nor is it beyond the reach of any one of us. If you get a thrill out of everyday living, find glory and romance in life itself, and do good work in your job, and then if you can do something to bring honourable fame, that is all to the good. But, by and large, the successful person is the one who — by the grace of God — gets the most out of himself.

How do you go about doing that?

Do Your Best

Many people fail to do their best because they are too intense. They live under pressure on the inside and thus press too hard on the outside.

I often remind myself of the late Branch Rickey, the leading baseball executive of his era, who was, at different times, chief of the St. Louis Cardinals, the Brooklyn Dodgers, and the Pittsburgh Pirates. He always insisted that a player must not press too hard. 'The secret,' he told his men, 'is to love the game. Go out and do the best you can, but don't try to get your name in the headlines. Don't over-press.'

I have found the same thing is true of making speeches — something I have been trying to do for long time. I made my first speech when I was about ten. That speech was made at the Bellefontaine, Ohio, Methodist church at nine o'clock one weekday night when nobody else was around. I went into the church, stood in the pulpit, and preached a sermon to a vast congregation that wasn't there. It was the greatest sermon ever delivered in the state of Ohio. And I was the only one to hear it!

I don't know much more about public speaking now than I did then. Every time I come onto a platform, I tighten up inside. I look out at the people, and they look at me — at least they are looking in my direction. And then I fight my battle to relax. I say to myself, 'You are not here to demonstrate how good you are. You are here to help people. Relax. Take it easy.' Any speech that is any good is a relaxed, easy speech. That does not mean that it has no fire. It does not mean that there are no high moments. But you must love what you are doing and never press too hard.

Create Positive Images

Imagination is one of the greatest skills known to man. We succeed by the images, the pictures, we form in our minds. No problem can overcome you if you think correctly about it. Suppose I lay an 18-inch- wide plank down in the middle of the street. Any one could walk up and down that plank, even run on it, without falling off. But if we raise the plank 25 feet above the ground, how many of us could get across? Not many. Why could you walk on the ground without falling off, and not up there? Because your imagination tells you you can, at street level; you have an image of yourself succeeding. At the higher level, your imagination tells you you cannot; your image of yourself is one of failure. That is a simple illustration, but it applies to any undertaking in this life. Get yourself an image that, with the help of God, you can do it. Print that picture on your mind until it becomes a part of your consciousness. Then you know you can do it.

Commit Yourself

If you commit yourself to Him, God will give you the power to do anything with yourself. But your belief has to be in-depth; no mere surface belief will suffice. It has to go down deep. To get the kind of power I am talking about, you must really believe.

Before World War II, Jimmy Go was editor and publisher of a big newspaper in Manila. He knew the Japanese had their eyes on the Philippines, so he started publicly opposing them. When the war came and the Japanese invaded the Philippines, the one man they wanted to capture was Jimmy Go. So, with his family, he took to the hills.

For three years, the Go family lived in the woods. Like animals, they had to grub their food out of the earth under the darkness of the night. Their hands became torn and tough. Time after time, they narrowly missed being found by the enemy. Many a night, they could hear the voices of Japanese search parties. The word was: Get Mr. Go! But after three years, the war was finally over and the Go family came down from the hills.

Years later, as I sat at dinner with Jimmy and his wife, I asked him, 'Jimmy, tell me, through all that critical time, how did you sustain your spirit?'

'I had my Bible,' he replied. 'It was all I did have. I read it so much that I almost know it by heart. And whenever I was troubled about what we should do for the slightest mistake could mean death — I read the Bible; and every time, God gave me a message. He guided me all the way.'

Not once in those three years of constant danger did God fail, because Jimmy Go was a believer.

What is Success?

What do we mean by the word 'successsful'? Who is the person who lives successfully? It is one who has solved the inner conflicts that have made him ineffective and unhappy. He is the person who has overcome the difficulties of life, risen victoriously over every obstacle; surmounted hazards; conquered the fears that plague men's lives; eliminated the hate and guilt that shrivel the soul. Such a person has learned to live with consummate success. It is the highest attainment of human experience.

What is the difference between Jimmy Go and some of us? He was completely committed. He really believed. He had such faith that he took God at His word.

Seek Opportunities

Have you ever noticed the way some people seem to attract opportunity? They are always getting new ideas, and new slants on life. Opportunities seem to flow to them, and they are surrounded by friends. They draw people to them by some irresistible magnetism, and actually bind people to them by ropes of steel. These attractive, successful, dynamic people are in every walk of life. They are among the famous and among the lesser known, but they are marked people because of this magnificent quality.

Then there are other people from whom opportunities always seem to fade. They are never quite able to get hold of life; it eludes them. They walk their ways lonely, misunderstood, longing for fellowship in the deepest sense. Why? Because one type has found the rare quality known as magnetic power; the others have missed it.

Is this magnetic power some gift granted by Almighty God to a favoured few? No. Anyone who is willing can program his mind to attract new opportunities and friends.

How do you do it?

Open Your Mind, Develop Your Personality

When our minds are alert and sharp, when our spiritual power is keen, we can grasp the opportunities hovering around us all the time. I believe that everyone has within himself the ability to see through any situation. The free-enterprise system, which has developed wealth out of many minds, is one of the greatest social systems in the world. It all depends on the degree of your mind's awareness to the situations around you.

Jesus was a simple man and He said simple things and He lived a simple life. But He drew all men unto Him. To a lesser degree, we can do the same. We can draw opportunities and friends to ourselves.

A person with a magnetic personality is filled with eagerness, vitality, enthusiasm; and these qualities are infectious. Nobody can resist them. The person who attracts either opportunities or friends always has these qualities. And if you do not have them, you can get them. Cultivate them by getting close to someone in whom these qualities are dominant. You will take them into yourself. To start, practice being magnetic, eager, vital, enthusiastic, and interested. See how it begins to galvanize life for you.

I once knew a baseball pitcher who practiced this vibrancy and happiness. When he came out onto the field, he would say: 'Hello, Lord! Thank you for this wonderful game of baseball. Thank you for my teammates. Thank you for my strong right arm. Thank you for my health. Thank you for the opposing players.' Then he added, 'I knew I was getting somewhere the day I could say, 'Thank you, Lord, for the umpire.'

This pitcher was a popular man in baseball and, because of his vitality, energy, and enthusiasm, constantly attracted new opportunities and made many friends.

We can do the same. Simply cultivate these habits: Do not talk negatively; do talk gloomily; do not talk cynically; do not talk pessimistically. Instead, think, talk, and act positively. Cultivate vitality in yourself and you will begin to attract people, because you will be attractive yourself; you will be eager; your mind will be alert and sharp; and you will see opportunities you have previously missed.

Discipline Yourself

Develop the ability to stand up under the difficulties of human experience and hold your temper, keep your good spirits, maintain your imperturbability. The person to whom other people turn is he who, when things are going bad, keeps his head, holds his spirit high, and continues to work with diligence and efficiency until accomplishment comes.

'But,' you say, 'I have trouble getting along with myself, so I have a hard time holding my temper and being in a good mood.'

Many people do.

Most of us will admit that we have been the cause of most of our trouble — although we often try to shift the blame to a spouse, a parent, a friend, a business associate, or to the Government.

There is a way to deal with these difficult personalities of ours. First, we must find out why we have so much trouble with ourselves. Ask yourself: 'Why do I do what I do? Why do I react in a certain way?'

I once visited with a woman in her nineties. She was healthy, wore no glasses, and would sit up half the night conversing with anyone.

'Why are you so vigorous and lively?' I asked her. 'What is your secret?'

'When I was a young woman and later, as a middle-aged woman, I lived in misery,' she replied. 'I was filled with fear of what I might do wrong. Every time I did

There was once a man...

There was once a man in Massachusetts who was hired to take marks off bills that had become smudged. He was given a big wad of cruder rubber with which to work. Sitting day after day, rubbing things out, he got to thinking. He figured that if he took a little piece of rubber and put it on the end of a stick, the work would be easier. Later, he had the idea of putting a bit of rubber on the end of a pencil. Now, every time you buy a pencil with an eraser on it, you are paying a royalty into his estate.

And there was another...

Then there was the man who had to hook up his wife's dresses everyday. Dresses used to hook from top to bottom, and he didn't like the job. It was most exasperating. He is the fellow who developed the zipper. He met a situation with a sharpened intellect.

anything badly, I criticized myself and dwelled on it and got angry. I finally decided that was a waste of time and energy. So I concentrated on the best of each minute as it came by. If I got things right, good. If not, I knew there was another minute coming.'

Isn't that wonderful? When unpleasantnesses occur, just keep going.

Do the best you can; grab the best of each moment and ask the Lord to help you do better next time. Move ahead. Take yourself in hand. Be master of yourself. Do not let yourself push you around — direct yourself. So many people fail at this. Self-discipline is one of the greatest accomplishments on earth.

Forget, Forgive, and Live

What is one of the most positive secrets of living life well? Naturally, in one chapter, I can only suggest an aspect of it. But, I want to share with you the philosophy of a man I know, who seems to have an extraordinary grasp of life, handling everything with skill and distinction. I asked him his secret, for I think every such person has a secret.

And this was it: 'Forget. Forgive. And live.'

Forget the Past

One of the hardest exercises known to man is to forget what has gone before. The tendency is to lug — that's a good word, it means to carry something heavy — into today and tomorrow all the mistakes and failures and frustrations and hates of yesterday. But eventually, you can't stand up under the load. You aren't strong enough. So learn to forget the past.

Did you make some mistakes yesterday? Of course you did. So did I, plenty of them. Extract from each mistake of yesterday whatever know-how it contains and forget the past.

Of course, no one likes to fail at anything. But, in due course, everyone will. And the question is what to do about it. Apparently, failure has been designed by the good Lord as an educational process. It is meant to teach us something.

John Henry Patterson

One of the wisest businessmen was John Henry Patterson, who developed the National Cash Register company in Dayton, Ohio.

I saw him once, when I was a young man, and always wished I might have known him better. He used to employ young men, giving them difficult and responsible tasks to see how they would handle themselves. He particularly watched to see how they handled their mistakes, saying that no one was any good who was afraid of making a mistake. Then he watched to see if they had quality of mind to overcome the mistake and do better the next time. Thus, Mr. Patterson surrounded himself with astonishingly competent businessmen; men not afraid to fail, men who could learn from their failures.

Forgive Yourself and Others

Did someone do you an injury, or say something mean about you, or treat you contemptuously yesterday? No doubt that could have happened. It may be just the right time now to consider honestly any resentments you may have, and practice forgiveness.

Then there is the matter of self-forgiveness. Did you commit a sin? And are you sorry for it? Hope you are sorry. Then forgive yourself. Don't let it linger in your consciousness as guilt, because if it does, it will burrow down into your unconscious mind and discolour your whole life. Get it forgiven and then forget it. Overcome your sense of guilt by two processes: first, by asking for, and receiving, God's forgiveness; and second, by forgiving yourself.

Live Today

God brings down a curtain of darkness every 24 hours to shut off the day that is past and to get you ready for tomorrow. Did you ever stop to think of the beneficence of the Lord in doing that? Sir William Osler, the great turn-of-the-century physician, said that we should live in 'day-tight' compartments. Each night, he said, we should pull down a great mental curtain, shutting out the past, and another great curtain, shutting out tomorrow, and go to sleep, unburdened by remnants of the past or anxieties about the future.

Suppose you knew that this is your last day on earth. What would you do with this day? How would you spend the remaining hours of this last day? Well, answer that and you will have answered how you ought to live every day. Wouldn't you want to pack it full of the greatest experiences — of love, goodness, fellowship, wonder, joy — every good thing?

Just as people brood about yesterday, they worry about tomorrow. But if you take care of today, tomorrow will take care of itself. So, forgetting those things that are behind, reach forward to those things that are ahead, remembering that your job is to be worthy, and God will take care of you. Having assimilated know-how from the past, live well today and you will come to tomorrow in the strength of right thinking and right living.

True Friends

Two men who had been lifetime friends had a falling out. Neither one would have anything to do with the other. They went to elaborate lengths to avoid each other. After several months, one of the men fell ill and was hospitalized. A mutual acquaintance persuaded the other man to visit his old friend.

'But I don't know what to say to him,' he protested.

'That's all right,' he was told, 'just act as if whatever had come between you was over, in the past, and forgotten.' It worked.

There is a healing in forgiveness. It mends broken relationships and makes everything new.

Cultivate Optimism, Don't Limit Yourself

Ralph Waldo Emerson once said: 'Nerve us up with incessant affirmatives. Don't waste yourself in rejection, nor bark against the bad, but chant the beauty of the good.'

God is good, hope and faith are essential factors in the attainment of the good life. If you cast out pessimism, and cultivate within your mind the attitude of optimism, miracles will take place in your life.

When you develop an optimistic attitude, tremendous resources are released within you. I doubt if anyone really appreciates the power that is in him, or her. Too many people have accepted the doctrine of limitation. How do you know you are limited? You *don't* know it! You have just accepted that negative idea about yourself. And, by so doing, you have limited yourself. The amazing power in each of us is so tremendous that none of us can fully comprehend it. So tell yourself that, through God, you have limitless power.

Get Outside Yourself

Late one night, I received a telephone call from a man in a nearby city. 'I just don't know what to do,' he said 'I'm so discouraged, I'm sunk. My wife is sick,' he continued, 'and tomorrow at three o'clock I have to meet the greatest crisis of my life. If things don't go right, I'm finished.'

'Listen,' I said, 'I have discovered that nothing is ever quite as bad as it seems.'

'I'm sunk,' he repeated.

'You will never get anywhere thinking like that,' I told him. 'If you are pessimistic, you will draw pessimistic factors to you. If you get optimistic, you will draw optimistic factors to you. The first thing to do is to stop concentrating on yourself. Let me ask you this, "Have you given anything to anyone lately?"'

'No, I haven't,' he admitted.

'Go to the Salvation Army tomorrow morning and give something to someone; forget yourself. Thank God that your wife is not dead — that she will get better. Be thankful that you are able to talk over the telephone, that you can eat your breakfast tomorrow morning. Thank God for the wonderful opportunity He is giving you tomorrow. And then pray for faith and hope. Practice expectancy and optimism. If you do this, things will turn out better than you think.'

I met him some time after. 'When I talked with you,' he said, 'I was dripping with gloom. I couldn't think.'

'Of course not,' I replied. 'No one can think when his mind is filled with negativism.'

'I did everything you told me to do,' he continued. 'But at that meeting, I got only part of what I wanted. However,' he added, 'later the results were better than anything I could ever have imagined. No one will ever find me depressed or pessimistic again. I'm a practitioner of optimism and faith. It clears the mind, clarifies any situation, and gets the power of God flowing through you.'

How right he is. If you are down about anything, pray enthusiastically, pray with thanksgiving. Do something for someone else. Get outside yourself. Get calm and quiet. And above all, flush out your mind with optimism. Think positively. Believe in the creative power of optimism, and it will work miracles in your life.

Think Health

I once asked a physician what he thought were physiological advantages of optimism over depression. This is what he said: 'Depression in the mind increases the possibility of infection by at least tenfold. Optimism, dynamic faith, has a power to burn out infection. You will notice people who maintain a confident attitude have a strange power in the presence of sickness and disease. I would recommend, as one of the great sources of health, an attitude of optimism and faith.'

This doctor's opinion has apparently been confirmed by a 35-year-long study completed only recently. Ninety-nine graduates of Harvard were interviewed, to determine who were pessimists and who were optimists. Analysis of their answers revealed that the optimists tended to respond to disappointments — like being turned down for a job — by formulating a plan of action and asking other people for help and advice. Pessimists more often reacted to such difficulties by trying to forget the whole thing or assuming there was nothing they could do to change things. Years later, according to a report in science journals, it was found that the men who had explained bad events pessimistically in early adulthood had substantially more illness at age 45 than those who had offered rosier explanations for bad events.

Now there is always someone ready to argue about the idea that thinking optimistically and practicing positive thoughts can affect your health. They will say, 'But I've got something really wrong with me.' We do not minimize organic disease at all. But even if there is something wrong, the forces of vitality and health can still be stimulated by how optimistically you think.

Consider a woman I called on at the hospital. After her husband had left the room, she said to me: 'I have cancer, but my husband is the real problem. He is in utter gloom all time, thinking depressing thoughts. Will you work on him and help him to think creative, positive health thoughts? I want him to see me as well, not as a victim of cancer or a wife he's going to lose. He isn't going to lose me, because I don't intend to die!'

I could have thought that this was like whistling in the dark, like talking big, because she was going to die. But when I looked into her eyes and heard her speak, I was convinced that this woman wasn't going to die.

'Don't worry about me,' she said. 'You don't even need to pray for me. Pray for my husband. Get him well in his thoughts.' Her husband and I got together, and we talked and prayed about it.

A long time later, I saw her in church — a dynamic, vital woman who walked down the aisle and asked, 'Do you remember me?'

'How could I ever forget you?' I asked, adding, 'you look very well!'

'Why,' she exclaimed joyfully, 'of course I'm well! I made up my mind that, with God's help, I would get well. And,' she added, 'Bill is thinking better.'

Thinking is a vitality-producing process. Think healthy thoughts. In so doing, you will keep your body in balance. You will keep it flowing in a normal, vital manner. If you think defeat, you will foster the circumstances that lead to defeat. If you think inadequacy, you will ultimately fail to perform in an adequate manner. But if you think victory and success — really think it, and believe it, *really* believe it — you will perform in a manner that leads to victory and success. See yourself as whole, the way God created you. See your body as clean, strong, and fine, and your mind in the same manner, the way God made it, and it will tend to be that way.

Talk, Visualise, then Listen

Do you want power in your life? Do you want insight, understanding, flashing intimations of knowledge otherwise denied you? If you fill your life full of God, and use prayer to put your problems into the hands of God, you will be relieved from all panic, all apprehension, all sense of defeat. That leaves you free to go out and do everything you can about the situation, free for a full application of all your power.

Think of prayer as a normal conversation between God and you. Open your heart and, in simple language, tell God how you feel and think. When you pray about something that means much to you, visualise it as being granted.

Always be willing to take what God gives. It may not be your desire, but it will be better for you than what you ask. He knows what is best for you. When you finish talking to God, relax your mind and body, become completely quiet, and listen for God to speak. Be receptive to His guidance and listen for His voice. It will come to you.

Believe in Miracles

Let me tell you about one of the most thrilling experiences of my life. After an evening address in a western city, I went to my hotel room to go to bed, for I was catching a plane at six o'clock the next morning.

The telephone rang and a woman's voice said 'There are about 50 of us waiting at my house for you. We are all praying that you will come.'

Before I could say no, two men were at my door waiting to escort me.

'We are a couple of alcoholics who have been changed by prayer,' they said. 'We have read your writings and you have helped us. We wanted to meet you.'

When we arrived at the house, there were about 50 people in a rather small room. One man was perched on a grand piano; many were sitting on the floor, on the stairs and on tables. A prayer meeting was in progress, and they told me there were 60 such groups meeting in that city every week.

I never was in a prayer meeting like it in all my life. They weren't at all a pious crowd. Suddenly, one would start to pray aloud, and I found myself strangely moved.

Then they would all burst into a hymn. I never heard such singing in my life.

Then one woman who had braces on her legs said: 'They told me I would never walk again. Do you want to see me walk?' And she went up and down the room; awkwardly, but still walking. She pointed to her braces. 'They, too, will go,' she said.

Then a fine-looking young woman got up and said, 'You know about drug addicts, don't you? I was one of them.'

And a man told of recovering from alcoholism.

A couple who had been separated by hate and infidelity told how they had come together again.

Then everyone burst into another song.

They wanted me to pray. We all held hands, and it was as if I had taken hold of an electric wire. I felt that I was the least spiritually developed person there. They had told me with modesty what they had been; I could see for myself what they had become.

You, too, can achieve everything you desire. Right this minute, go look at yourself in the mirror. Say to yourself, 'I am a being with infinite perfectibility. With God's help, I can begin again. There is no limit to what I can become!'

And then start applying the positive action principles.

Chapter 8

Trust
believe in yourself
believe in the future

Self trust is the first secret of success.

— *Ralph Waldo Emerson*

$\mathcal{I}$t seems to me that the events of recent years have turned many of us into worriers. We worry about our children, our communities and our world.

Sometimes we even worry that there might be worries we haven't thought of yet.

The answer to our quandary is simple: 'Depend on the Lord, trust in Him, and He will take care of you.'

Throughout the ages, those who have trusted in the Lord have prevailed.

Thank God for your problems, rejoice in them, for you are never more alive than when, with God's help, you call on your creative power to solve them. Trusting in God to be with you as you meet the challenges of our times is your foundation for creating secure future for you and your loved ones. Remember: God has created you in his image, and his power is within you. Trust that God has given you the power to meet the challenges of our times, and you will find peace.

Optimism

Do you know why I truly believe in positive thinking? It is very simple: because our Lord does. He teaches that if you want to accomplish something, you must see a vision of your goal materialising. If you have faith, amazing things will happen to you. You must keep out of your thoughts all negativism. Instead, trust in the Lord, dwell in the positive.

Live in the way that you know in your heart that God would want you to. Give your best to your family and your work. Be honest, sincere and frugal; be conscientious, treat people right and all times trust and believe in God. Do this and life will come to you rather than elude you. You will live abundantly.

∼

When I was a small boy, my brother Bob and I sometimes visited our grandparents in Lynchburg, Ohio, for a few days. One night after Grandma had put us to bed, a terrible storm came up. The wind whirled furiously around the house, and rain was hurled in great sheets against the windows. From my bed I could see a huge maple tree that I knew to be a hundred years old lashing back and forth in the fury of the storm.

Terrified, Bob and I scurried downstairs and cried out to Grandma, 'The big tree! It's going to go down.'

Grandma calmly bundled us up and took us out on the porch. 'Isn't it great to feel the rain on your face?' she asked. 'Isn't it good to get out here in the wind? God is in the rain and the wind. Just look at that tree having a good time in the storm, yielding to it, bending one way or the other. It is playing with the storm, and it will be there for a long time to come. Now, you go to bed, boys. God is in the storm, and all storms ultimately pass.'

Grandma was right about the tree, of course, and she gave me a philosophy about storms. You are not going to be immune from life's storms, but they pass. When they come, don't surrender to fear. Instead, put them and yourself in God's hands. Relax in the Lord, as the wisest of men and women always have, and wait for Him to make your way smooth.

Conviction

Never forget that you are God's creation and that, as His son or daughter, He wants the best for you. But remember, you must respect His desires for you by matching them with your own. Only with a deep desire can you attain your highest goals. If the desire to attain your goal is operating at full strength in your mind, you are moving toward achieving it.

Don't let adversity or setbacks discourage you. Let them teach you, season you, help you to find a better way, just like all those who succeed have had to do. Believe in God, believe in life, believe in yourself and in your future. That is the secret of creative living. Keep faith in yourself and in God. God didn't design you for failure. He wants the best for you.

We are told that God takes note of every sparrow that falls and even numbers the hairs on our heads. The least among us is very important to God. So make sure that He is as important in your life as you are to Him. Every day say aloud, 'I am a child of God. God is interested in the smallest detail of my life. God loves me.'

Let nothing that happens today, or has happened before, discourage you about tomorrow. The happy fact is that what has troubled you today may tomorrow work for your good. Because God loves you and is always with you, you can have confidence that if you live His way to the best of your ability and put your trust in Him, nothing can defeat you.

Harmony

There is such a thing in this universe as divine harmony, and we are intended to be part of it. When our priorities are right and we stop thinking about ourselves and get to loving other people, when we appreciate what a privilege it is to live and how much there is to enjoy in our lives and, above all, when we commit our way to the Lord and trust in Him, then He, in wonderful ways, will bring harmony into our lives.

Most of our problems come from conditions within ourselves. We borrow trouble; we fear the unknown; we doubt our abilities. No one says you have to think this way; how you think is your choice. Instead of dwelling on your problems, try the divinely simple advice of the old hymn: 'Count your blessings, name them one by one.'

If you want to conquer fear, don't
sit at home and think about it.
Go out and get busy.

— *Dale Carnegie*

Not long after I got in his taxi, the driver recognised me and asked if I would like to hear a story of the time he met God. It was in the aftermath of World War II when he was a little boy in battle-ravaged Holland. In Rotterdam food was so scarce that people dug up tulip bulbs to eat.

'One day,' he told me, 'a notice from our pastor went around saying that there would be a meeting in our church. It was the only hope we had. The big church was packed with two thousand people. There was no sermon. The pastor prayed. People prayed aloud all over the church.

'All of a sudden, I became aware that God was right there. I could feel Him in my heart. I knew that He was going to take care of us poor starving people. Then we sang some hymns and went out into the streets and back home. With a gnawing, empty stomach, I fell asleep.

'Early the next morning we were awakened by the roar of an armada of airplanes over Rotterdam, and there began a great shower of food being parachuted down to the streets. We ate, and we were saved.' The driver glanced back from his taxi's front seat and said, 'As long as I live, I will believe that God heard our prayers and, out of His great heart, He fed His children.'

And, because He is a loving God, I do believe that God answered the prayers of those 2,000 in Rotterdam. You are His child, and He takes care of His children. Return His love and trust in God with all your heart. This trust will lead you to peace in times of trouble.

Success is not a matter of money.

Providence

Here we are on this earth, a whirling island in the sky. Our lives are in the hands of Someone who directs its orbits and laws. Each day we get up and go about our affairs without giving this much thought. Implicitly we trust in God to keep our planet spinning peacefully in the universe. It follows that if you trust Him in all things, He will take care of you. Whatever your circumstances, you can be sure that God watches over you. You can be confident that you are never out of His sight or His loving concern.

Don't forget to thank God for watching over you. After every journey thank Him for His protecting care. Do the best you can in your daily life and leave the outcome to God. Confidently trust Him to handle things beyond your efforts.

Constancy

Thoughts of good will, trust, confidence and goodness create a spiritual calm and help you relax. Do not make the mistake of thinking of God as far away and removed from this earth. He is with you right where you are at this very moment. The Scriptures promise that even if you 'dwell in the uttermost parts of the sea' God will be with you.

John Masefield, the onetime bartender who became Poet Laureate of the British Empire, renewed himself each evening by what he called 'the getting of tranquility.' He would lie down, sing a hymn or recite a few lines of poetry, then say quietly, 'God is with me; God watches over me.' As you walk along on your way to lunch or an appointment, form the habit of repeating, in your own way, this same assurance

Wherever you go, take God with you as your companion. Make God your partner in life, and you will dwell in the house of the Lord forever.

Personal Notes

Personal Notes

Dear Reader,

Welcome to the world of **Orient Paperbacks** — India's largest selling paperbacks in English. We hope you have enjoyed reading this book and would want to know more about books published by us.

There are more than 700 books on a variety of subjects to entertain and inform you. The list of authors published include, amongst others, distinguished and well-known names such as Arun Joshi, Anita Desai, Bhabani Bhattacharya, Dr. S. Radhakrishnan, R.K. Narayan, Mulk Raj Anand, John Buchanan, Shakuntala Devi, Khushwant Singh, Greg Chappell, Dr. O.P. Jaggi, H.K. Bakhru, Norman Vincent Peale, Robert Schuller, Windy Dryden and Paul Hauck **Orient Paperbacks** truly represent the best of Indian writing in English today.

We would be happy to keep you continuously informed of new titles and programmes through our monthly newsletter, **Orient Book Review**.

SMS your **name** and **full address** to **99112 26733**,
and we will regularly send you
Orient Book Review completely **FREE** of cost.

Available at all leading bookshops | **Orient Paperbacks**

www.orientpaperbacks.com